The
CRM
PROJECT
MANAGEMENT
HANDBOOK

For my wife Christine, and our children
Kevin, Marina and Steven

The
CRM
PROJECT
MANAGEMENT
HANDBOOK

**Building realistic
expectations and
managing risk**

Michael Gentle

**KOGAN
PAGE**

London and Sterling, VA

First published in Great Britain and the United States in 2002 by Kogan Page Limited
Reprinted in 2003

120 Pentonville Road
London N1 9JN
United Kingdom
www.kogan-page.co.uk

22883 Quicksilver Drive
Sterling VA 20166-2012
USA

ISBN 0 7494 3898 3

British Library Cataloguing in Publication Data

A CIP record for this book is available from the British Library.

Typeset by Saxon Graphics Ltd, Derby
Printed and bound in Great Britain by Biddles Ltd,
www.biddles.co.uk

Contents

133; Leave integration out of a pilot 135; Be flexible about whether to do UAT 135; How to choose a pilot group, site or country 136; Limit an international pilot to a single country 138; Chapter summary 139

Acknowledgements

Before becoming an author, I never used to pay much attention to the Acknowledgements section in books, which I sometimes called the 'friends and family' section. I'd either take a quick glance at it, looking for familiar company names, or ignore it altogether.

Now with this first book, I've found out what all other authors already know, namely that producing a draft manuscript is one thing, but turning it into a finished product is quite another. The plain truth is that manuscripts, usually replete with poor grammar, logical inconsistencies and technical inaccuracies, would never become books without the assistance of others.

To start with, let me thank my twin brother and fellow author Robert Gentle, who inspired me to try my hand at it as well, and who helped to draft the killer proposal in the space of a weekend.

Then there are the reviewers, all CRM and business professionals in their field, who had the unenviable task of finding time in their already-busy schedules to read critically through the manuscript and not only highlight inconsistencies and areas of disagreement but also round off some of the rough edges of my sometimes cynical and flippant writing style (and I'm not sure which of the two was the more difficult). So many thanks to:

▮ Howard Hughes, CRM consultant from Ciberion in London, who managed to devote quality time to the manuscript while shuttling between London and Geneva on a CRM project.

▮ Bill Jago, CRM consultant in London, who had a particularly keen eye for my rough edges, and additionally went out of his way to provide several paragraphs of detailed input on a number of subjects, which he then allowed me to reproduce integrally as part of the book. These cover the 'waterfall' approach, customer affiliations, international CRM projects, pilot projects and offline usage with synchronization. When Bill writes his first book, as I'm sure he will, I hope I will be able to return the compliment.

▮ Rogier van der Male, Technical Account Manager from Siebel Systems in the Netherlands, with whom I worked for almost three years. Rogier's experience in the trenches, so to speak, of many CRM projects helped to validate the main theme of this book.

▮ Dr Alain Micaleff, Head of Worldwide Clinical Safety and Pharmacovigilance at Serono International in Geneva, who provided essential business-level feedback, and helped to validate one of the case studies in which he played a major role in his previous company.

▮ Xavier Pourrier, Programme Manager for an international CRM project at Biogen in Paris, who was able to review the manuscript critically less than a month before implementation of his CRM project.

▮ PRISM team members Philippe Conrardy, Olivier Gavalda and Christopher Woods for their contributions, and the rest of the PRISM team at Worldcom, whose outstanding performance contributed directly to many of the lessons in this book.

▮ Tom Rohm, member of PA Consulting's management group in Paris, who provided essential executive-level feedback.

Finally, I would also like to thank the following editors for allowing me to reclaim both text and style from articles I had previously written for them in the mid-90s as a guest columnist, when I was still honing my writing skills:

▮ Mitch Betts at *Computerworld* for the following: 'Find out if you're a US-centric IS manager' (1996), 'Sales force automation:

you'll know you're in trouble when...' (1997), 'Titles and departments we could do without' (1998).

▌ Dale Agger at *iSeries NEWS* for the following: 'No free lunch' (1993), 'Real-world package selection' (1993).

▌ *Datamation* for the following: 'Be a local hero' (1994).
Copyright INT Media Group. All rights reserved. Used with permission.

Last, but not least, special thanks to the team at Kogan Page, who helped to bring this book to market so quickly: Stephen Jones, Fiona Meiers and Emily Steele.

List of abbreviations

ADSL	asynchronous digital subscriber line
BPR	business process re-engineering
B-to-B	business-to-business
B-to-C	business-to-consumer
CEO	chief executive officer
CFO	chief financial officer
CIO	chief information officer
CRM	customer relationship management
ERP	enterprise resource planning
FAQ	frequently asked question
ISDN	integrated services digital network
IT	information technology
JAD	joint application design
kbps	kilobits per second
LAN	local area network
MAN	metropolitan area network
MD	managing director
PABX	private automatic branch exchange
PDA	personal digital assistant
PTT	post, telephone and telegraph

RAD	rapid application development
RFP	request for proposal
ROI	return on investment
SFA	sales force automation
SME	small or medium enterprise
SOHO	small office, home office
SoR	statement of requirements
WAN	wide area network

Introduction

NOT ANOTHER BOOK ON CRM!

There are at least 101 books on Customer Relationship Management (CRM), whose basic message goes something like this (fill in with the theme music from *Star Trek* for maximum effect):

> *CRM – the final frontier...*
> *These are the voyages of the enterprise...*
> *... its five-year mission (a not unreasonable time-frame)*
> *... to explore brave new words (like retention, loyalty and up-selling)*
> *... to seek out new life and new customers*
> *... to boldly go where no company has been before!*

Hey, beam me up, Scotty!

Though useful for an understanding of CRM, most such books are ultimately 'MAP' books, ie Motherhood and Apple Pie. In this ideal world, companies have radically transformed their processes and systems to serve the cause of our noble customer, who is now firmly in the driver's seat. And since these 'MAP' books gloss over the practical difficulties of project execution and delivery, it is virtually impossible not to put your hand on your heart and pay allegiance to the new paradigm.

And yet, 80 per cent of all CRM projects either fail outright or do not deliver significant business benefit. So clearly, the world doesn't need another 'MAP' book expounding on how great CRM is and why everyone should be doing it. What we *do* need is a book to help cut through the hype and explain how to do it right, so that you in turn don't become yet another accident statistic.

WHY THIS BOOK?

Once you've bought into the concepts of CRM (difficult not to!), how do you separate the practically useful from the pie-in-the-sky, and then actually put it in place? Given the high visibility of CRM and the intense pressure to go out and get it done before the competition, you'd expect a sizeable amount of literature and guidance on the subject, wouldn't you?

Sadly, there is very little available. Unless you have the time to surf the Web and pull together the right information, the most common way to launch a CRM project today seems to be to buy a few thousand licences of the latest whiz-bang technology, and then write a blank cheque to a systems integrator or consulting company.

Since I first started working on CRM projects in 1993, I have personally witnessed some spectacular, multi-million-dollar failures that resulted from just such an approach. I have also witnessed some spectacular breakthroughs and successes that cost 10 times less, resulting from an entirely different approach. Lessons from both the successes and the failures are covered in this book. From these experiences, I identified a list of dos, don'ts, how-tos and gotchas for successfully launching and managing CRM projects. The result is this book.

WHAT THIS BOOK IS

This book identifies the critical success factors and risk factors for CRM projects, regardless of vendor, product or technology, and regardless of your industry or sector, and proposes practical solutions to get round them.

The emphasis is on how to approach CRM in the real world, ie the one with ineffective processes in which the customer hardly figures, performed by people who resist change or have always done it that way, and who are then rewarded based on the output of those ineffective processes. Then throw in some organizational, cultural and political baggage at management and executive level, stir well and that begins to describe the real world you are probably also familiar with. Naturally, if your particular environment does not correspond to the above, then you may close this book without a second thought (though you won't get your money back!).

Lastly, this book is about 'operational CRM', which is transactional and takes place 'live' in the customer-facing areas of sales, marketing and customer service. This is in opposition to 'analytical CRM', which takes place 'after the fact', and seeks to understand customer behaviour by analysing the information aggregated from operational CRM systems and back-office systems. This focus on operational vs analytical CRM is deliberate: they are two entirely different areas, and the former is a prerequisite for the latter.

WHAT THIS BOOK IS NOT

This book is not about CRM as a concept, ie managing customer relationships with a view to making your enterprise more profitable. Neither is it a how-to book, with a step-by-step methodology for running CRM projects. There are very few such books anyway, mainly because implementation methodologies are usually in the domain of vendors, systems integrators and consulting companies.

Lastly, it is not a catalogue or guide for technology, products or consulting services. There are therefore no names or direct references to vendors, products or consulting companies. This is not because there aren't any good ones, but simply because the critical success factors and risk factors identified are independent of these third parties.

WHO THIS BOOK IS FOR

This book is for all those constituents with a vested interest in building realistic expectations for CRM and managing the associated project risk:

▌ the CRM project manager in a company, and related decision makers and influencers;

▐ key business executives at the front line in terms of results (sales, marketing and customer service directors) and funding (finance director);

▐ vendors, consultants and integrators, so that they can be on the same wavelength as their clients.

It can be used at any phase of the project – feasibility study, launch, implementation, post-implementation, though of course the earlier the lessons are applied, the better.

Part I

Building a realistic foundation for CRM

1

Overhyped, overpriced and over here

The truth will set you free – but before it does, it will make you miserable.

(De Marco's dictum)

EVERY WHICH WAY BUT EASY

Anyone who has navigated the jumble of CRM definitions and product offerings has probably felt like a mouse lured into a maze containing small morsels of every conceivable kind of cheese (Computerworld, 1993). For many senior executives, CRM is the ultimate competitive edge, which will allow an enterprise to identify, capture and retain its most profitable customers, cross-sell and up-sell to them through multiple channels, and provide true satisfaction and loyalty in the process. Information technology (IT) sees it as an exciting new technology that will at last restore credibility and have the user community beating a pathway to its door. And the poor sales rep is stuck in the middle wondering: if CRM is the answer, just what was the original question?

CRM is certainly a sound concept, which has gained a lot of ground, but it has been hyped and oversold to the point where many people in the industry tend to see the tools and technology as ends in themselves, and underestimate the complexity of process and organizational change. Four out of five CRM projects either fail outright or do not deliver significant business benefit. CRM is like teenage sex: everyone's talking about it; few are doing it; fewer still are doing it right.

In this chapter, we will show that:

▌ The very high failure rate of CRM projects can be attributed mainly to a lack of 'due diligence' on the part of the companies launching them. There are clearly identified critical success factors and risk factors, which are almost exclusively related to the companies themselves rather than to the vendors and consultants.

▌ Pundits have portrayed CRM as an instrument for survival, requiring the radical transformation of people and processes at great expense. These are impossibly high stakes, and do not correspond to reality or to what is feasible in a general business environment trying to make its numbers for the year.

▌ The complexities of organizational change necessary to implement CRM successfully are so far-reaching that the learning phase will still run for a number of years before we begin to see acceptable results in sufficiently large numbers.

▌ The experiences of business process re-engineering (BPR) and computer-aided software engineering (CASE) 10 years ago show that strategic and all-embracing concepts that are supposed to transform the enterprise radically can often prove extremely difficult and frustratingly elusive. Strategic CRM used in this manner is clearly in this category.

INTO THE TROUGH

For those familiar with the Gartner Group's famous hype cycle (see Figure 1.1), CRM has already passed the 'peak of inflated expectations' and is now clearly in the 'trough of disillusionment'. This cycle occurs repeatedly in the field of information technology, eg PCs, client/server, CASE, BPR, enterprise resource planning (ERP) and now CRM. The hype cycle is an extremely helpful and factual observation of how new technologies and concepts move from the pioneer phase through reality check to mainstream. It helps us to understand what's going on and to view things constructively. With this in mind, let's see how CRM got to its present state.

In the late 1990s, industry pundits got out their crystal balls and officially sanctified CRM. According to them, it was going to transform bland, single-channel, product-oriented companies into sexy, multi-channel, customer-centric companies with the ability to sell to profitable and loyal customers on the back of seamlessly integrated processes and systems. Of course, would-be pioneers soon discovered that getting departments like marketing, sales and customer service to change their processes and share information, and then getting all those disparate systems talking to each other, was easier said than done.

Numerous studies and surveys from very reputable companies (Forrester, Gartner, Hewson, Insight, IDC, Meta, Standish and others) show the very limited success rates of CRM projects. No matter how you slice it, only around 20 per cent of CRM projects can be termed a success. Why is this so? Are we dealing with rocket science here? Is the gap between theory and practice so great that a long and costly phase of trial and error is required before being able to produce reliable and repeatable results?

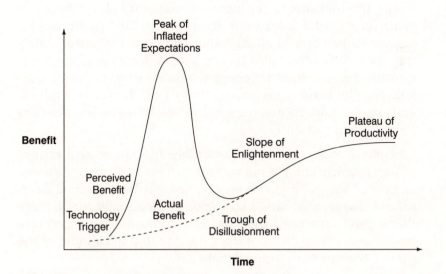

Figure 1.1   *The Gartner hype cycle*
Source: Gartner Research (Gartner Copyright)

The answer to this is a resounding 'Yes!' – just as it was for PCs, client/server, CASE, BPR, ERP and any other technology or concept you can care to name, when they were still in the pioneer phase and moving through the hype cycle. We therefore have to accept that CRM must also go through a learning phase. And this means understanding the critical success factors for CRM, and the risk factors that represent potential failure points.

WHY CRM HAS FAILED SO ALARMINGLY TO DATE

The very high failure rate for CRM projects can, in the main, be attributed to: 1) not taking into account some basic (and some admittedly not-so-basic) IT and business principles for launching the project in the first place; 2) coming up post-launch against one or more potential failure points, which then spiral out of control, taking the project with them.

Here's a summary of the most common problems, which will be examined in greater detail in subsequent chapters:

▌ *Lack of a clear business case and objectives*, ie a recognized and identifiable business problem to solve, and measurable benefits to justify the investment (eg decrease customer churn by x per cent; shorten the sales cycle for product ABC to six weeks; answer 80 per cent of all customer enquiries without transferring the caller). Most CRM business cases don't stand up to real scrutiny, because they are either too flimsy to be really measurable (eg 'increase sales productivity') or too fuzzy and all-embracing really to mean anything (eg 'achieve 100 per cent customer satisfaction').

▌ *Lack of active sponsorship* to articulate the above and ensure project momentum. It is not enough to have an executive's name associated with a project; there also needs to be a full-time director or manager reporting to the sponsor to actually run it. Since this is rarely the case, the executive sponsor soon becomes a figurehead whose distance from the day-to-day running of the project ensures its eventual demise.

▌ *An IT-led project.* When IT is the main driver, the project assumes a technology focus rather than a business focus, and is then presented to the business as an IT project instead of a business benefits project. This diminishes user buy-in. A lot of CRM projects are IT-led, though this is not always an attempt by IT to want to be in the driver's seat. The business also mistakenly sees CRM as being primarily about systems and technology, which explains why a figurehead executive sponsor (previous point) is quite content to turn over the running of the project to IT.

▮ *Thinking of CRM as a system.* Most companies have the impression that CRM is mainly about installing systems and technology. There's no such thing as a CRM system, at least not in absolute terms, as for example a spreadsheet or a word processor, which you can install and start using straight away. It's a business concept, linked to business processes, and adequately supported by systems, technology – and people. (Qualifier: for convenience, we will nonetheless use the term 'CRM system' or 'CRM solution' when referring to packaged solutions from 'CRM vendors'.)

▮ *Lack of organizational readiness for CRM.* Certain prerequisites in terms of organizational and process maturity must be in place for CRM to happen. Otherwise it's like trying to get the company to run when it hasn't learnt how to walk properly. When projects are launched under such conditions, the original CRM objectives are quickly shown to be unattainable until the required maturity has been reached. These prerequisites can take a year or more to achieve, effectively suspending the original project.

▮ *An unrealistically wide project scope.* Because CRM spans the enterprise, there is often a tendency to want to deliver results across multiple functions from day one, eg for both sales and order management. This represents a Herculean challenge in terms of people, processes and systems, which is more realistically managed via a phased, modular approach. CRM is ultimately a journey, not a destination, and needs to be planned with realistic milestones that take into account the complexities of the terrain and the uncertainties of the road ahead.

▮ *Insufficient change management resources* within the business to nurture the solution once it is in place, ie to define training from a business perspective, to drive process change and ensure data quality. This is mistakenly thought of as 'IT support', and insufficiently budgeted for. When reality finally dawns, it is usually too late to obtain the required funding within the current budget cycle. The business is therefore unable or unwilling to provide the people for this critical function.

▌ *No buy-in from end users.* Executives and management (who rarely use the system) mistakenly assume that end users will be naturally motivated to take up CRM because it makes sense, is good for the customer, the company, etc. In reality, users have jobs to do, which they usually perceive as having nothing to do with CRM, and will only accept a new tool and new processes if they deliver tangible benefits that make their current jobs easier. This is especially true for the sales force.

▌ *Signing a blank cheque to systems integrators*, and expecting them to do the job. While integrators and consultants can and do deliver value, the client has a huge responsibility for creating and sustaining the conditions under which this will occur. At best this is seriously underestimated by the client, and at worst totally ignored. This once again ties into the mistaken perception that CRM is all about putting a system in place, and hence the idea that you can outsource it to an integrator and come back three to six months later when it's ready.

▌ *Organizational change and company politics.* Companies don't start CRM projects; people do. These dynamic visionaries are often the key to successful projects. However, the realities of company politics mean such people are usually unable or unwilling to find allies at executive level. So once the sponsor moves on after the umpteenth executive reorganization, and tangible results are not yet visible, the initiative almost always dies a natural death.

▌ *Absence of a proper operational pilot* of sufficient duration (two to three months) to be able to validate the business objectives, obtain buy-in from end users, and identify and correct the real-world problems that only show up when used in a live environment. Many projects start off as either a big-bang implementation or a pseudo-pilot, ie a first phase with no option for backtracking. Such projects stand a high chance of ending up in damage-control mode from day one, and then either fail outright or are suitably descoped in order to meet deadlines, regardless of the usefulness of the deliverables.

▌ *Poor data quality*, usually the result of years of data neglect in legacy systems, which not surprisingly are unable to provide clean data for migration to the new CRM system. Then, to make matters worse, insufficient resources from the business are assigned to data quality, which soon goes from bad to worse. Unless rectified very quickly, usage drops below a critical level, which can then only be resolved by starting the implementation and training phase all over again, with the inevitable loss of credibility and 'mind share' this implies.

▋ *Complex international projects with little business justification.* International CRM projects are frighteningly expensive and fraught with complexity, both technical and organizational. They should therefore have a justifiable business case based on cross-border services that require international data sharing at transactional (as opposed to reporting) level. Yet many companies not in this category launch international CRM projects for reasons like 'international reporting', 'standardized processes' or 'cost reductions through international synergy'. While certainly useful as secondary objectives – when at all possible – they cannot be cost-justified as primary business drivers.

▋ *Poor international project management.* International projects are usually perceived in subsidiaries as being imposed by HQ and run with a 'big-stick corporate project' mentality, which places insufficient emphasis on country buy-in and local realities. This inevitably leads to rejection from subsidiaries, who in many cases are not even asked to approve the corporate solution.

▋ *Using the traditional 'waterfall' or 'cascade' method*, ie the rigidly contractual, life cycle approach, which takes over a year to produce any meaningful results. This usually occurs when the project is managed by an IT department with little or no experience in software packages. While this approach might be appropriate in different settings and for other types of projects, it is clearly inappropriate for CRM, which is essentially a moving target. And moving targets are best handled as part of an iterative process, with three- to four-month cycles based on workshops and a prototype.

▋ *A request for proposal (RFP)-based approach*, ie a long-drawn-out process in search of the holy grail, based on a 'statement of requirements' (SoR) weighing in at a few hundred pages. This is then followed by the detailed customization of the chosen product to correspond to the exhaustive requirements in the SoR. Though the final deliverable theoretically corresponds to 'requirements', in practice it is often unusable.

▌ *The complexities of offline usage.* Most CRM packages allow the sales force to use a laptop offline in disconnected mode, and dial in to the network at their convenience to synchronize with the central database. In many cases, the business benefits of working offline with a laptop (as opposed to a handheld device like a PDA, or Personal Digital Assistant) are exaggerated by the sales force, for whom it is usually a convenience more than anything else. However, the technical complexity and business constraints associated with this mode of working, especially in a highly volatile data environment, can quickly bring a CRM project to its knees.

▌ *IT resisting organizational change.* Resisting organizational change is usually seen on the business side, as it comes to grips with the realities of CRM. However, the same phenomenon can be observed in some IT departments. Traditionally, IT is structured by vertical function, eg a silo for sales, another for order entry, another for customer service etc, each responsible for a vertical system. As a customer-facing function, however, CRM requires an IT organization with a horizontal component – which cuts across traditional boundaries and fiefdoms. This could lead IT to lean towards solutions that are biased more towards its internal organization than to the CRM business requirement.

ARE VENDORS AND CONSULTANTS TO BLAME?

But surely, you must say, the above issues are hardly new. Some of them are applicable to any project, and CRM has been around for a few years now. So why is it that they have only been seriously raised since early 2002? Well, actually, people *were* talking about them – on Web sites, at CRM seminars, at vendor–user conferences, during consulting briefings etc. However, it was a problem of timing: you did get to hear about them eventually, but usually only once your project was already under way. By then it was too late to do anything but try to anticipate and correct problems on the fly.

You mean that the vendors and consultants actually know all this? Of course they do. They've seen it played out time and time again, and can probably add some more items to the list. (This book assumes that the norm for CRM is to buy software packages rather than build in-house solutions, and to rely heavily on consultants rather than on in-house staff. We do not take application service providers (ASPs) into account either, because at the time of writing they are not yet sufficiently mainstream.)

So are they selling us a false bill of goods, or lying by omission? Well, let's run through their sales pitch and find out. For the vendor:

▮ The product *does* work as shown in the demonstration (even though the demonstration was conducted by a product expert who doesn't correspond remotely to the level of Joe or Jane User).

▮ It *can* be up in the space of a few weeks (provided your processes don't deviate too much from the plain vanilla or 'out-of-the-box' version, and assuming you know what your processes are).

▮ It *can* be customized (which can take days, weeks or months depending on how far you deviate from plain vanilla).

▮ It *can* enable your sales and marketing departments to share accounts and contacts for prospects and customers (if it's agreed beforehand who owns the data, who purchases it, whether new data can be entered or updated after purchase, and by whom, who ensures the information is valid and coherent, etc).

▮ It *can* enable your sales force to share information with other players in the sales cycle, and close deals in a fraction of the time it took them before (assuming their existing processes are the same as the package's processes, and the degree of customization isn't too great, and all the players agree to change their way of working).

▮ It *can* virtually eliminate invalid orders through the use of a product configurator, knocking days or weeks off order processing time, and decreasing time to revenue accordingly (assuming marketing, sales and order entry work from identical product definitions and product codes, and that the business rules for pricing, order configuration, billing etc are documented and agreed by all).

▮ It *can* allow any of the customer-facing people in your company to give a customer the status of an order (assuming there are processes and people in place to do this, and that the back-office systems that process the orders have this information, and are interfaced to the CRM system).

▌ It *can* enable your service rep in the call centre to have access to cross-channel customer information, and to provide astounding service, and cross-sell and up-sell in the process (assuming there are processes and people in place to do this, and clearly defined groups of people responsible for providing this information and maintaining its quality, especially if parts of it originate from other systems).

▌ Even if it's expensive in absolute terms, if it *can* do all of the above, it is a bargain in terms of ready-to-roll features and time to return on investment (ROI).

For the consulting company:

▌ They *do* bring to the table their knowledge of enterprise-wide processes and systems, and how CRM can benefit a company (assuming the company has reached the required stage of organizational and process maturity for this to happen).

▌ They *do* have the skilled resources the client usually lacks, and an implementation methodology that can produce rapid and reliable results (assuming that all the conditions and prerequisites are met, especially the availability and commitment of key business resources during the requirements and configuration phase, and that the processes to be built into the new system have been reviewed, validated and correspond to reality).

▌ They *do* cost an arm and a leg, but if they can do the above in the short time they claim, they are a bargain in terms of time to ROI.

Well, running through this list, I would say there are no false claims, either by the vendor or the consultants. I'd even go as far as to say that not only are the underlying assumptions reasonable, they go without saying. What's more, almost all of the issues concern the client and the client's organization, not the vendor's product or the consultant's services.

Vendors and consultants might be guilty of a lot of other things, for example a mistaken conviction of the simplicity of their products, and a naivety of how difficult it is to bring about people and process change in the real world. But they're certainly not guilty of duplicity and selling false claims about their products and services – no more than are vendors who sell hardware, ERP software and database systems.

Yes, everything is indeed possible – but hardly likely. And that's the crux of the matter – the products and services are sold based on a series of assumptions that exist only in an ideal world. The real world, as we all know, is something entirely different.

OK, so that still means it's their fault, doesn't it? After all, if they pointed out all these realities in their sales pitches, we'd think twice before launching such projects. Would we really?

Let's try to imagine hypothetical vendors giving their pitch, but this time round trying to point out all of the above in a noble attempt to prevent CRM from getting a bad name. And since almost all of these factors concern the client organization, the vendors don't have to worry about incriminating their own product, which works as advertised. So at strategic points in their presentation, they try to point out factors that could lead to project failure. For example:

▮ 'You don't have an executive sponsor? Well, we would highly recommend that you do, because experience shows that…'

▮ 'We notice that most of the people in this room are from IT. Who are your points of contact in the business, because our experience shows that…'

▮ 'In reply to your question, "What is this thing called change management we refer to so often?", it means simply that…'

▮ 'You say that marketing is not part of this first phase of the project, and that all they need at this stage is the ability to use the system to replace their existing Access database, which you're sure they'll accept because of all of the additional benefits possible. Well, at the risk of being out of line, our humble recommendation is that you get them into the loop.'

▮ 'Now that you've seen the benefits of the product configurator, we must nonetheless point out that, for any of this to happen, your marketing, sales and service delivery must work from a common set of product and pricing rules.'

OK, I think you get the point. Any vendors who adopt this type of approach will almost certainly expose themselves to one or more of the following reactions:

▮ Unspoken: 'What do these people take us for – amateurs? Can't they mind their own business and stop telling us what we must and must not do?'

▌ Unspoken: 'These people are a bit too patronizing for my liking. Do they really think they have to preach to us and treat us like beginners with no prior project experience? Do I really want to work with this company later, with them as teacher and us as students?'

▌ Unspoken: 'Really, I didn't know all of that. If this is true, then we're really in trouble. We probably shouldn't have launched the project the way we did. Maybe we should just call the whole thing off.'

▌ Spoken aloud: 'We appreciate your attempts to point out certain things to us based on your own experience and those of other customers, but we have managed projects of similar size and scope before, and are therefore well aware of the organizational and other prerequisites that we will have to deal with. At this stage I therefore think it would be better if you kept your demo focused on the product and what you need to do, and let us worry about what we have to do. Thank you.'

Even if they use the most diplomatic language, any well-intentioned vendors who try to increase awareness of the complexity associated with CRM risk being seen as overstepping the mark. At best, they'd be insulting people's intelligence by telling them things they already know, and at worst they'd be calling people's level of professionalism into question. What you can be reasonably sure of is that hardly any prospect is going to back out of CRM as a result, or even hold off for a while. If such an approach does result in fewer sales for the vendors, it will most likely be because the prospect prefers dealing with other vendors who have a better 'attitude'. You can run through a similar scenario for a consulting company and come to the same conclusions.

DUE DILIGENCE: IS IT THE CLIENT'S FAULT?

So, the high failure rate of CRM is not the fault of the vendors and consultants, much as that conclusion would appeal to many of us. So who do we blame for this mess? Well, if it's not the vendors or the consultants, it can only be ourselves. You, me – the client! It's called due diligence, and is the full responsibility of the client. *Caveat emptor*, or 'Buyer beware', has never been more true than it is today for CRM.

So it's the client's fault? Well, if you asked this question a few years ago, when CRM was more or less in its infancy and all these lessons were being learnt on the 'bleeding edge', then the answer would have been 'no'. You can't assign blame so easily for lessons that were not common knowledge at the time.

In the new millennium, however, the answer is clearly 'yes'. Those who go into a CRM project today without exercising due diligence beforehand clearly have no one to blame but themselves. There is sufficient published research on the subject, and enough people to talk to (other companies who've been through it before, specialist consultants – even the vendors if you ask them).

Now why do seemingly responsible people like you and me fail to exercise due diligence when it comes to CRM? For the very same reason we buy a thousand and one other things in life, from cars to cosmetics: consciously or subconsciously, we buy into an evocative and enticing vision of how things could be if the promises made in the ads and demonstrations could only come true for us. Even if we do decide to take some precautions, we are rarely objective: we tend to focus on those 'findings' that support our desire to purchase, and can always find ways around those that should urge caution.

Vendors, of course, know all about this – the vision and the promise are paramount, regardless of the assumptions and prerequisites necessary to attain them. With very generous help from consultants, research analysts and the press, CRM vendors have put together an enticing vision of CRM destined for the business community, with the promise of radically transforming the bottom line of the enterprise. Of course, the underlying messages used to trigger product interest are not as frivolous and unsubtle as those normally used to sell cars and cosmetics, namely the increased health and wealth of the consumer, combined with a high level of popularity with members of the opposite sex. No, as CRM is a much more serious subject, the corresponding messages have now become the increased health and wealth of the enterprise, combined with a high level of popularity with its customers.

The basic message normally encountered can be broken down as follows:

∎ CRM is the ultimate competitive edge, which will allow an enterprise to identify, capture and retain its most profitable customers, cross-sell and up-sell to them through multiple channels, and provide true satisfaction and loyalty in the process.

▌ Look how (via a combination of product demonstration, vendor white papers and testimonials from reference clients) our CRM product can help your company to achieve a competitive edge, or at least begin to tap into its enormous potential!

▌ By using our CRM product, your company can also be a part of this brave new world. And by the way, your competition may have already embarked on this process, or will be pretty soon, so it could become a question of your survival in the market place. So there's no time to lose.

▌ And yes, we have many clients, but because of confidentiality we can't say who they are.

With such an effective marketing message, most of us let our guard down. And when the presenter puts up the inevitable slide with all those customer logos, you can be forgiven for thinking that you've somehow missed the boat. So now you too have 'gotta have it', simply because your major competitors have it – even though you've no factual information on how it has changed their lives and made them more successful. After all, can so many prestigious companies be wrong?

Like any good advertising message, this one is based on the truth and makes no false claims. However, it is also very much based on assumptions and prerequisites without which the vision and the promise cannot be realized.

IMPOSSIBLY HIGH STAKES

Once any good concept or technology comes along in IT, you can be sure it will be picked up by consultants, research analysts and the press, built up, developed, dissected and before long blown out of all proportion. This is the first curve of the hype cycle (see Figure 1.1, page 9), which leads to the famous 'peak of inflated expectations'.

These expectations are so great that reason and healthy scepticism end up taking a back seat to urgency and the need to move forward. What starts off as an interesting concept with a lot of potential, which you might want to look into but which certainly won't affect the survival of your enterprise, soon ends up as the final frontier, which you ignore at your peril – and that of your company.

Just how successfully companies have bought into this picture can be seen from the massive growth of the CRM market in the period

1998–2000, which saw it move from concept through paradigm through instrument for survival. It has been oversold to the point where not to be on this particular bandwagon can almost be seen as a dereliction of duty. I personally know of a billion-dollar company with an IT department with so much money on its hands that it earmarked a few million dollars for 'a CRM project' in 2001, regardless of the fact that there was no demand for it from the business.

And the method put forward for getting from here to there is for the chief executive officer (CEO) and the board to sit down with consultants to understand the benefits of CRM, analyse the complete operations of the company, work out a road map, acquire the appropriate technology and products, and then transform the company to reap those benefits.

This would already represent a Herculean task for small, single-site companies with a hundred employees and a single product line serving a very specific market segment. Yet the majority of those targeting CRM are million- or billion-dollar companies with thousands of employees over multiple locations, and multiple product lines serving multiple market segments. Just how do you get such a mass of people, processes and systems to achieve the incredible transformation that CRM implies, while at the same time ensuring they don't drop the ball and go out of business altogether?

The analogy that comes to mind is that of a football team of average ranking, positioned in the middle tier of the league, which decides in mid-season to adopt a radically new approach that would take it to the undisputed number one position at the top of the league. This new approach, which is based on strategy and tactics that are foreign to most of the players, is applied during subsequent training sessions and will be gradually implemented over the rest of the season. During this time the coach will have to get the players to accept change and play by the new rules – but without changing any of their contracts, because that can only be done at the end of the season. But most importantly, the coach has to do this in such a way that, if the approach doesn't yield the desired results right away (official statistics show only a one in five chance of success), the team at least maintains its current position and doesn't end up losing a string of matches, which could see it drop to the bottom of the league or even face relegation to the second division.

These are impossibly high stakes. For vendors, consultants, research analysts and the press to put forward such a radical programme for change in the business landscape – and moreover to link it to the very survival of the companies concerned – is unrealistic. It ignores the fact that in the real world companies have products to introduce, markets to conquer, market share to grow, sales targets to meet, customers to service and a share price to grow. Anything that causes them to blink, or to take their eye off the ball, has to be managed in terms of risk.

It also ignores the fact that, in the real world, Joe and Jane Customer are just normal people like you and me. They bear little resemblance to the exacting customers portrayed in CRM literature, who hold their vendors to the highest possible standards imaginable, demand to be delighted with outstanding products and stellar service at every turn, and are ready to jump to the competition at the click of a mouse. I'm sorry, but I just don't buy it. Below a certain dissatisfaction threshold, the norm is 'better the devil you know', ie your average customer will want to avoid as far as possible the hassles involved in changing vendors, and having to go through another learning cycle. In today's commercial environment, which comprises products and services of a distressingly wide quality range and fairly average after-sales service, all customers want is a reasonably priced product that meets expectations, understandable and error-free invoices, and prompt and effective handling of service issues and general enquiries. Simply by meeting, never mind exceeding, these expectations, companies will already get rave reviews and be well on their way to CRM.

CRM as advocated by the pundits today seems to be based on radical change bordering on revolution. And as we all know, revolution is incompatible with business as usual (as anyone who lived through the days of BPR and CASE can attest to – of which more later).

The realistic route to CRM would seem to be via evolution, one step at a time. Despite all the talk about CRM being strategic and requiring CEO leadership, practical reality says that CRM is ultimately a step of intelligent tactical initiatives, which may or may not lead to the strategic vision.

B-TO-B, OR BACK TO BASICS

The overselling of CRM, which has resulted in the current 'adapt or die' situation, has also unwittingly generated the message that CRM is ultimately about being the best. To succeed in CRM it is not sufficient to be marginally better or to show consistent progress over time – you have to be in the finals. The only game in town is the one that will allow the select few to gather round the table to share the spoils of victory.

Whether you're playing football, basketball or tennis – at high school, university or professional level – CRM says that if you want to be taken seriously (nay, if you want to survive), you have to aim for the World Cup, the NBA finals and the Grand Slam circuit, regardless of whether it's remotely within your reach. Even if you can dramatically improve your current game at your particular level, no matter, your performance will now be judged against that of David Beckham, Michael Jordan or Venus Williams.

To aim for the stars or reach for the sky is of course fine and necessary when it comes to motivation and inspiration. But this should not be confused with actual, achievable results. CRM in its current state is not only trying to motivate companies to reach for the sky; it is also holding them accountable for achieving this, without which they're not even considered to be in the race.

In reality, however, each company, just like each individual tennis player or football team, has a different starting point in its particular league. From this starting point, progress can then be measured – not on the way to CRM perfection, but on the way to achievable milestones within that league, for example qualifying for the championship, or reducing by half the number of goals conceded this year compared to last year.

Similarly, the vast majority of companies in the world have the potential to improve on a whole variety of metrics across the enterprise (marketing, sales, service), which can have a significant impact on customer retention and the bottom line. Even basic telephone training and teaching people to be more courteous to customers and to return calls within 24 hours – let alone being able to find the right person in the first place – would result in a quantum leap in customer satisfaction, and in terms of results would qualify as part of CRM.

By such incremental but consistent improvements over time, these companies, just like the tennis player and the football team, eventually reach the stage where they're ready to play in the big league. Once this stage of organizational and process maturity is reached, then big-ticket CRM of the type advocated today would become a realistic possibility. Until then, they should be concentrating on the basics through process improvement, adequately supported by either existing systems or new systems – which may or may not be related to CRM.

BREAKING THE BANK

The costs of CRM are significant in absolute terms: anywhere from US $3,000 to US $15,000 per user per year. Big-ticket implementations weigh in at around US $8,000–15,000 easily, and can go as far as US $20,000–30,000 depending on the degree of dependence on consultants and integrators. In one pharmaceutical company, for example, a near-exclusive dependency on a big-X integrator for an international CRM project resulted in a total cost of US $30,000 per user for the first year. Ditto for a global petrochemical company, with a first-year price tag of US $35,000 per user for just one country. And both these examples were limited to the sales and marketing functions.

In relative terms, however, eg when factoring in the bottom-line impact of reduced customer churn, shorter sales cycles, improved forecasting, reduced time to revenue etc, such costs may be acceptable – indeed, they may even represent small change. However, if you're not realizing such benefits, then there is an equally important bottom-line impact in terms of money down the drain.

Let us try to quantify this by imagining a CRM implementation in a fictitious 500-person company with a combined front-office staff (marketing, sales, sales support, order management and customer service) of 250. Applying the rather generous figure of US $5,000 per year for each of the 250 users, that yields an annual CRM cost of US $1.25 million.

If the annual front-office staff cost is averaged out to US $50,000 per person per year, then the US $5,000 per year cost of CRM for each user represents a 10 per cent increase in their annual cost. Each front-office employee using CRM software would now cost US $55,000 per year.

While any cost must of course never be viewed in isolation but always in terms of the expected benefits, it would nonetheless be useful to see what else we could do with US $1.25 million. For example, instead of spending the money on CRM, we could use it to increase the front-office staff numbers. With front-office staff costing US $50,000 per year, US $1.25 million would enable us to hire another 25 people – or a 10 per cent increase in headcount over the original 250.

Now I am by no means advocating increasing headcount instead of spending money on CRM, which in any case also needs a valid business case. But at least it is an option companies are comfortable dealing with, eg increasing the sales force by 10 per cent can be expected to yield measurable benefits.

Imagine yourself now going to your CEO and recommending a 10 per cent increase in the annual cost of your 250-strong front-office staff, to the tune of US $1.25 million – and then saying that this money is not going to be used to hire 25 more people, because you don't believe the ROI justifies it, but will instead be used to implement something called CRM, with potentially a much better ROI, but unfortunately one that you can't really guarantee (at best an even chance of success, at worst one in five).

Needless to say, you have to be well prepared. For some excellent examples of the types of questions you could face from the board or the CEO when trying to present a business case, refer to the section entitled 'Proving the ROI case' in the book *Carving Jelly* (Siragher, 2001: 70).

SPEND FIRST, THINK LATER!

In 2001 I attended the annual European User Group conference of one of the leading CRM vendors. During a breakout session on customer success stories, a vice-president (VP) from an international telco was lamenting the fact that not enough forethought goes into CRM projects. After reviewing some of the common mistakes they had made (eg too many features for day one, an IT-driven project, insufficient sales force buy-in etc) and had to correct before the project started to yield benefits, he put up a slide entitled 'Think first, spend later!', which recommended the approach they would take if they were to start all over again.

I put up my hand and begged to differ, stating that, while in theory that made sense, in practice the real thinking starts only once you get into trouble and have a real problem – and to get into trouble, you first have to spend money! So in reality it's actually the other way round, ie 'Spend first, think later!'

Psychologists say that until you reach a certain pain threshold, you are not sufficiently motivated to take the steps necessary to fix a problem. Pain doesn't have to mean agony, but simply any form of discomfort that has a personal impact you can no longer ignore.

This is why it is so difficult to get healthy people to stop smoking: despite abundant evidence that it is a dangerous habit, the real motivation to change is usually triggered only once it starts to affect you personally, eg you start coughing after climbing a flight of stairs.

The same is true in business. Moving from a vertical, function-oriented organization with little or no information sharing, to a horizontal, process-oriented organization with information sharing as required by CRM, is a complex and 'painful' process with enormous people, process and system issues. Though the pain can be reduced somewhat by careful planning and forethought, it must ultimately be experienced first-hand before people are able really to start thinking about ways to overcome it.

Now I am by no means suggesting you don't think before spending, or that you spend money on software licences and consultants and launch a project without forethought. Obviously, you need to do it intelligently, but the chances are that your major lessons will be based more on your own experiences than on those of other companies. This will then form the basis of your subsequent thinking.

It could be argued that the best candidates (I'd even go as far as saying the only candidates) for CRM are those who've already been burnt, and have consequently seen the light. The following saying should be hung up on the wall of the executive sponsor in every company embarking on CRM: 'You will die, you will pay taxes and your first attempt at a CRM project will not yield the expected results.'

BPR – BACK TO THE FUTURE

By now it should be pretty clear that CRM is not about technology but about people and processes, adequately supported by technology. For those of you who've been getting a sense of *déjà vu* while reading this chapter, you're not alone.

Around 10 years ago, business process re-engineering or BPR became the dominant concept in IT and business. CASE and client/server, the other buzzwords of the day, were discreetly removed from centre stage, and the book *Reengineering the Corporation* by Hammer and Champy (1994) replaced Tom Clancy novels as required reading for both business and IT executives on summer vacation in 1993.

Consultants, research analysts and the press suddenly discovered decades after the modern corporation was formed that the internal functioning of certain departments was often based on objectives that were too narrowly defined. Taken to extremes, this could result in a perverse logic that rewarded the wrong things, to the detriment of the big picture – and plain common sense.

One of Hammer and Champy's examples concerned an airline that had a plane with a technical problem. The required spare part was readily available in a regional warehouse near the airport where the plane was stranded, but the local manager was not 'incentivized' to remove parts from 'his' stock to help out. So the plane sat on the ground until the part was flown in the next day from the plane's home base. The regional warehouse manager was simply basing his actions on the narrowly defined objectives that applied to his budget. BPR would not have allowed such a situation to happen, because the big-picture objective of keeping the plane flying and generating revenue would have taken precedence over any locally defined operational objectives. And all parties would have been 'incentivized' based on these big-picture objectives.

The objective of BPR was to change a company's processes to make them more coherent from an enterprise perspective, and less perverse from a departmental perspective. This would be done by first taking an existing high-level process (eg order collection) and breaking it down into its constituent sub-processes. Each sub-process would have:

▌ one or more players responsible for its execution (usually employees from one of more functions of the enterprise);

▌ one or more inputs (eg a fax or a phone call) from various players, whether internal (employees) or external (vendors or customers);

▌ a transformation (ie what is actually done by the players, eg calling up the customer to verify incorrectly entered information and then entering the order in the system);

▌ one or more outputs (eg a valid order, plus a fax confirmation to the customer).

In most companies such processes are not even documented, since they are rarely the direct result of any high-level thought on the subject, but more an evolution of the work methods of various people in the organization over time. And more often than not, the final picture is one of an ineffective set of processes crying out to be streamlined. Once documented, these processes would be reviewed from a non-departmental, cost-effectiveness perspective, and then re-engineered to eliminate or optimize those sub-processes that don't add value.

This was all well and good. However, once you stripped away the big picture, common sense, cost-effectiveness and all that, the main driver for BPR was cost reduction – alas in the form of reduced personnel. Of course, this didn't ensure the wholehearted coopera-tion of the people involved. This was one of the main obstacles to the success of BPR projects, which became the corporate equivalent of the TV programme *Survivor*. Then followed a spate of downsiz-ing and lay-offs in the recession of the early 90s, some of which was attributed, rightly or wrongly, to BPR.

Needless to say, this signalled the end of this particular buzzword. It was the way BPR was applied and its perception as a front for lay-offs, rather than because of anything intrinsically wrong with it, that caused the problem. After all, if the early 90s had experienced a boom characterized by hiring, instead of a recession characterized by lay-offs, then the resources freed up by BPR could have been suitably redeployed, and Hammer and Champy would have been canonized.

However, just because BPR stopped being the buzzword *du jour* didn't mean it died out as a concept. After all, the principles remained valid. So a part of the corporate world quietly carried on applying the principles – but on a smaller scale and taking into account the human factor – in order to improve business processes, because it made sense from a cost perspective – and from a customer perspective (shades of CRM to come).

Today people hardly use the term 'BPR', preferring instead the more neutral terms 'process re-engineering' or 'process restructur-ing' or 'process mapping' or 'process definitions'. Whatever the term used, BPR is now an integral part of the landscape, as witnessed by its acceptance today as a prerequisite for CRM.

Though the re-engineered processes usually required adjust-ments to existing systems and sometimes the installation of new ones, BPR was primarily seen as a business issue rather than a tech-nological issue. After all, there was no such thing as a 'BPR system' or a 'BPR vendor', unlike CRM today.

However, the *déjà vu* that hits us here is that CRM is ultimately BPR applied to the front office (marketing, sales, service), suitably linked to the back office, and adequately supported by technology. Unravelling customers from these departments so that they can be viewed and handled as enterprise assets, as required by CRM, can only be done by changing the processes – ie by BPR. This is an inescapable reality for anyone dealing with CRM.

What should also be an inescapable reality is that the greater the scope of the CRM effort, the correspondingly greater will be the underlying BPR effort. Re-engineering processes within a single department, or at the boundary with another department, is one thing; doing it at the level of the enterprise is another thing altogether. After all, we know how difficult and elusive enter-prise-wide BPR proved 10 years ago. The real-world experience of BPR therefore seems to be saying that strategic, all-embracing CRM stands less chance of success than a series of tactical CRM initiatives.

CASE AND CRM – A FUNDAMENTAL ANALOGY

In the late 80s and early 90s, the IT world was abuzz with a hot new technology called CASE (computer-aided software engineering), which is remarkably similar to CRM in terms of its journey through the hype cycle (Figure 1.1, page 9). As we will now see, CASE also allows us to understand better the challenges facing CRM.

CASE was to bring to IT the same productivity and quality bene-fits seen in other computer-aided (CA) technologies like CAD/CAM (computer-aided design/computer-aided manufacturing). Certainly, around this time IT was still plagued by its legendary woes: high costs, low returns, eternal maintenance, dissatisfied users.

The basic premise was that systems development was a semi-manual process involving teams of programmers who were basi-cally artisans and craftspeople. This was expensive and time-consuming, and needed to be suitably automated, ie computer-aided, to make it faster and more cost-effective.

If you already know about CASE, you can skip the following introduction and go straight to the next section.

A layperson's introduction to CASE

In the coding or programming phase, the 'manufacturing' part of IT, the main tool was a programming language (eg COBOL) with a set of basic instructions (eg read, write, add etc) that enabled programmers to build systems for the business. This approach had two main downsides. Firstly, it was time-consuming because the limited vocabulary, or instruction set, resulted in programs with hundreds or even thousands of lines. If English had a similarly limited vocabulary, then instead of saying to your dog Rover 'Fetch!', you'd have to say 'Watch me; see where stick lands; run in direction of stick; stop at stick; pick up stick; return to me.' Secondly, since everyone writes programs based on their own logic and thought processes, it is not always easy for other programmers to understand. This means that whenever another programmer has to modify a program for whatever reason, and the original programmer is no longer around, the resulting 'maintenance' can take many times longer, depending on the complexity of the program.

If we were to use house building as an analogy, then instead of builders using standard components with standard assembly instructions, they would make their own and assemble them according to their own techniques. The end result might still be a safe house, but under the surface no two houses would be alike in terms of structure and components, and any repairs would be very difficult for people other than the original builders.

Prior to coding, the design phase – the 'architecture' part – was also a completely manual process, carried out in an artisan manner. Data modelling, which is the equivalent of the architect's drawing plans and diagrams, was fairly rudimentary – when it was done at all. Database design, eg which files or tables would hold customer data and order data, and how they would relate to each other, was not done according to proper design principles – or was done on the fly and built up over time. This was acceptable for simple systems but proved disastrous for more complex ones. A skilful builder who had learnt the trade on the job with a minimum of training might be able to build a small, single-storey house, but if that builder tried to wing it with a more complex, multi-level mansion, the outside might look perfect but structurally it would pose problems after a few years, or earlier if you wanted to add extensions. The resulting design errors would have a knock-on effect on everything that followed, resulting in costly corrections once the system was installed. Studies at the time showed that an error captured early in the design phase could be corrected at negligible cost, but once it found its way into the coding phase, it would already cost three times more to fix, and if undetected until actual usage would cost 10 times more to fix in the maintenance phase.

Enter CASE, which was supposed to transform IT from artisan status to industrial status by:

- enforcing design principles through data modelling;

- introducing standard 'components' and 'templates';

- providing a more intelligent vocabulary for the programming language.

This was supposed to result in:

- robust design because of data modelling principles;

- higher productivity through shorter programs (you could now use just one instruction, 'Fetch', to ask Rover to get the stick, and a 'code generator' would automatically generate the six underlying instructions);

- easy-to-maintain code, since everyone would now work from standard components and templates understandable by all, instead of trying to figure out someone else's twisted logic.

The resulting productivity and quality would enable: 1) the delivery of systems to the business in a much shorter time and at much lower cost; 2) a shorter maintenance phase for changing business requirements.

The analogy between CASE and CRM

CASE vendors proposed tools to handle either the design phase ('upper-CASE') or the coding phase ('lower-CASE'), or sometimes both within a single tool ('full-CASE'). The sales pitch was resolutely silver-bullet, ie by purchasing these tools an IT department could bring itself from the artisan age into the industrial age, and transform its tarnished image to that of a credible and fully fledged partner.

Alas, and here begins the analogy with CRM, there were some major unstated assumptions. Just as most of the users targeted by CRM are not customer-aware, most IT departments were not software-engineering-aware: 1) In the design phase, if you've never done data modelling with a pencil and paper, you're not likely to be able to do it with a tool. CASE would make this phase mandatory.

2) In the coding phase, programmers were being asked to forgo the 'creativity' that led to their individual works of art and instead become more 'disciplined' by assembling pre-built components.

Whereas the IT director and managers had no problem buying into CASE, whose *raison d'être* was articulated in terms of benefits to the business, the same was not true of the IT staff who actually had to use the tool, mainly the programmers. Just as for CRM, IT execs and management mistakenly assumed that their staff would be naturally motivated to take up a software engineering approach because it made sense, and would be good for IT and the business. But taking up software engineering would effectively result in abandoning the old ways of working, and starting afresh with a new approach. All the experience accumulated to date would not necessarily be an advantage – in fact, it was usually the contrary: newcomers less encumbered by baggage could actually adopt the new approach more quickly than their more senior colleagues. So, at the end of the day, as with CRM, we ended up with a concept that held great promise at executive and management level, but that staff had great difficulty buying into.

Also, an IT director couldn't migrate the whole IT department to CASE without dropping the ball on other projects. So invariably the successful introduction of CASE was first done on a pilot basis, with a limited number of staff on some small projects that served as a test and proof-of-concept for the rest of the department. There were also some spectacular fiascos, with some IT departments gambling on big-bang introductions of CASE applied directly to major projects.

Those IT shops that succeeded introduced CASE on a pilot basis, with a mix of new staff and retrained existing staff; they also inevitably had to let go those unable or unwilling to work under the new regime. But they succeeded in transforming their organizations and reaped the benefits: end-to-end development cycles and costs reduced by a factor of three or more were not uncommon (my personal experience).

Table 1.1 summarizes the similarities between CASE and CRM in terms of the difficulties of introducing them into the organization.

Why did CASE meet with limited success? The reasons above could be summarized as follows: everyone was so hung up on the technology and the tools (the CA – computer-aided – part) that they overlooked or underestimated the underlying concepts (the SE – software engineering – part). In other words, before you can be

Table 1.1 *A comparison of CASE and CRM*

	CASE	CRM
Radical transformation/new paradigm with enormous potential?	Yes.	Yes.
Initially perceived as a silver bullet: all you needed was to purchase the technology to reap the benefits?	Yes.	Yes.
Population targeted by vendors and consultants	Executives, directors and managers.	Executives, directors and managers.
Direct benefits to accrue to	The business.	The business.
Indirect benefits to accrue to	IT department.	The customer.
Benefits generally clearly understood by	Top management.	Top management.
Benefits generally not clearly understood by	Non-management staff (programmers).	Middle management (sales managers) and non-management staff (sales force).
In order to work, buy-in essential from	Non-management staff (programmers).	Middle management (sales managers) and non-management staff (sales force).
Main prerequisites for buy-in	An understanding of software engineering, and how it ultimately benefits the business.	An understanding of the customer's viewpoint, and how it ultimately benefits the business.
Radical departure from existing work methods?	Yes.	Yes.
Resistance to change from	Non-management staff (programmers).	Middle management and non-management staff (users).
Non-management users appropriately incentivized to use new system?	No – assumption made that they would naturally buy into CASE.	No – assumption made that they would naturally buy into CRM.
Big-bang transformation possible to new paradigm?	No – otherwise IT department would drop the ball concerning its other commitments.	No – otherwise the business would drop the ball concerning its other commitments.
Main criteria for success?	People first buying into a new concept, and then applying the appropriate technology.	People first buying into a new concept, and then applying the appropriate technology.

computer-aided, you first have to be a software engineer – or, put another way, 'A fool with a tool is still a fool'. Asking people to adapt to a new tool plus a new job is asking for too much. The tool can only come after they've bought into the new job.

Having said that, CASE never really died as a concept; after all, the principles remained valid. Though the technology stopped being a growth industry, a part of the IT world quietly carried on applying the principles in order to reduce the development cycle – but with more common sense, ie placing the appropriate emphasis on data and process modelling first, and the tool second. Today hardly anybody uses the term 'CASE'. The attention has now shifted to process modelling and data modelling. And most of the development tools in use today produce code directly from data models.

In conclusion, those in IT who remember the challenges faced 10 years ago in trying to introduce CASE should now be able to project themselves into the business and see how CRM is facing many of the same challenges. When CASE succeeded, it did so at a tactical level (clearly designated projects) rather than at a strategic level (all IT projects across the board). The real-world experience of CASE seems to be saying that strategic, all-embracing CRM stands less chance of success than a series of tactical CRM initiatives.

CHAPTER SUMMARY

We can summarize this chapter as follows:

∎ CRM is a valid business concept with enormous benefits for both a company and its customers. However, it has been hyped and oversold to the point where many tend to see the tools and technology as ends in themselves, and underestimate the complexity of process and organizational change.

∎ The very high failure rate of CRM projects can be attributed mainly to a lack of due diligence on the part of the companies launching them. There are clearly identified critical success factors and risk factors, which are almost exclusively related to the companies running the projects rather than to the vendors or consultants providing the products and services.

∎ CRM as advocated by pundits today is nothing less than an instrument for survival, requiring the radical transformation of people and processes at great expense. These are impossibly high stakes and correspond neither to reality nor to what is feasible in a general business environment.

▌ The complexities of organizational change necessary to implement CRM successfully are so far-reaching that the learning phase will still run for a number of years before we begin to see acceptable results in sufficiently large numbers. And as each company is different, such results will usually be contingent upon the lessons learnt from a company's own previous CRM initiatives.

▌ The experiences of BPR and CASE 10 years ago show that strategic and all-embracing concepts that are supposed to radically transform the enterprise can often prove extremely difficult and frustratingly elusive. Strategic CRM is clearly in this category, which should indicate caution and lead us also to consider the more realistically achievable approach of tactical CRM.

After a brief introduction to CRM, the rest of this book draws on the themes covered in Chapter 1 to create a list of critical success factors and risk factors for CRM, which are then summarized into a 40-question risk analysis. Finally, the book ends with three case studies (two successes and a dramatic failure).

2

CRM 101 – just the basics please

If a company lost 10 per cent of its inventory, it would react very quickly. But if it lost 10 per cent of its customers to the competition, it probably wouldn't even be aware of it.

(Lefébure and Venturi, 2001)

You could grow old trying to agree on a definition of CRM. It's an evocative concept that means different things to different people. Whole books have been written on CRM and how it can benefit the customer and the enterprise. The challenge here is to summarize the basics to provide a framework for the rest of this book, and not to treat you to yet another author's spin on the subject.

The emphasis is therefore on the basics, with no attempt to qualify the exceptions of this or that sector to which some of the generalizations would not apply. A key example is the pharmaceutical industry, with its complex mix of players and intermediaries, in which even the term 'customer' is relative and can refer to either the doctor or the patient.

THE CUSTOMER LIFE CYCLE

At the most simple level, a company deals with a customer through three basic stages (see Figure 2.1):

▌ 'sales', which covers all activities from identifying and targeting potential customers (ie marketing), to first contact, to a commitment to buy, and finally to contractual closure;

▌ 'delivery' or activation, installation or implementation of the particular product or service;

▌ 'after-sales' or service management, which covers those activities concerned with the ongoing relationship, like billing, customer service and general enquiries.

This simplified model assumes a one-way street, in which the relationship is based on a customer who continues to use the original product or service bought through to the end of its useful life or the end of the contract. In reality, of course, it is a circular relationship, which can cycle back to the sales phase with the customer buying more – or other – products or services. So the complete customer life cycle is shown in Figure 2.2.

PROCESSES ACROSS THE CUSTOMER LIFE CYCLE

Within each of these three stages, there are a number of processes. These can be internal to the company, eg defining customer

Figure 2.1 *The three-stage customer life cycle (simplified)*

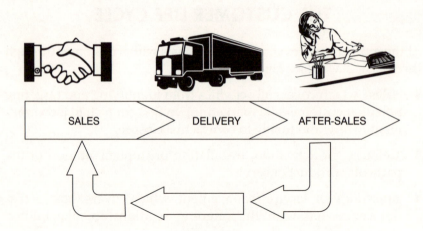

Figure 2.2 *The three-stage customer life cycle (full)*

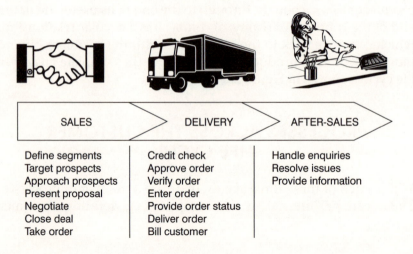

Figure 2.3 *Customer life cycle processes*

segmentation or purchasing data for a marketing campaign, or external, eg providing the customer with the status of an order or handling a billing inquiry. See Figure 2.3, which shows these basic high-level processes. Note we are not concerned here with back-office processes like finance and ERP.

Though usually easy to describe at a high level, these processes can be fairly complex behind the scenes, and involve multiple players from multiple parts of the organization. For example, the high-level sales processes can be broken down into their constituent functions and sub-processes (see Figure 2.4). These sub-processes can in turn be further broken down to a level at which the players and the actual tasks can be analysed and evaluated (not shown).

MARKETING	SALES
Purchase new data	Prepare call
Qualify new data	Manage activities
Analyse customers	Analyse requirements
Define segments	Update contact details
Define campaign	Prepare proposal
Execute campaign	Manage sales force
Handle responses	Update funnel for forecasting
Generate leads	Present proposal
Set appointments	Negotiate
	Close deal
	Take order

Figure 2.4 *Detailed sub-processes for sales*

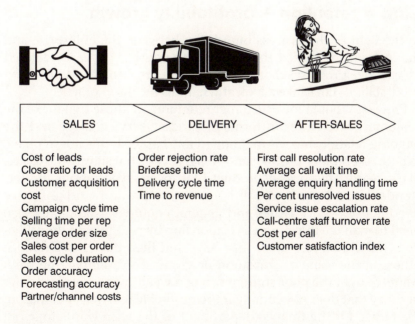

SALES	DELIVERY	AFTER-SALES
Cost of leads	Order rejection rate	First call resolution rate
Close ratio for leads	Briefcase time	Average call wait time
Customer acquisition cost	Delivery cycle time	Average enquiry handling time
Campaign cycle time	Time to revenue	Per cent unresolved issues
Selling time per rep		Service issue escalation rate
Average order size		Call-centre staff turnover rate
Sales cost per order		Cost per call
Sales cycle duration		Customer satisfaction index
Order accuracy		
Forecasting accuracy		
Partner/channel costs		

Figure 2.5 *High-level process metrics across customer life cycle*

PROCESS METRICS

The above processes can be measured and evaluated based on three criteria:

▌ importance, ie how important the process is to the customer or the company;

▌ effectiveness (or doing the right thing), ie to what extent it is the 'right' process – one that makes sense and delivers value, regardless of its efficiency (next point);

▌ efficiency (or doing it right), ie to what extent the process is being 'properly' done in terms of speed, output or throughput, regardless of its effectiveness (previous point).

By applying these metrics to the processes in the customer life cycle, we can get an idea of how effective a company's processes are. Figure 2.5 shows some of the high-level metrics associated with the basic three-stage customer life cycle.

CRM FROM A COMPANY PERSPECTIVE

CRM = retention + profitability growth

In the light of the process interaction between the enterprise and the customer discussed above, CRM can now be very easily defined as 'effective processes that favour customer retention and increased profitability'. Let's take a look at what this means in practice.

Processes that favour customer retention are those that make the customer's life easier in terms of product/service usage and the ongoing relationship. As mentioned in Chapter 1, this doesn't have to be an exemplary product and stellar service but simply the basics, like a reasonably priced product that meets expectations, understandable and error-free invoices, and prompt and effective handling of service issues and general enquiries. Companies also need to manage the ongoing relationship by recognizing the affiliations individual customers may have and their power to influence others in the same organization or group. For example, the bank wants to treat the poor student son of a wealthy business customer in a way that does not endanger the profitable revenue stream from the father. Or the finance department of the telco wants to avoid disconnecting the private data service at the home of the corporate customer's managing director because the invoice was sent to the wrong address or was chewed up by the managing director's dog.

Once a customer perceives a company as not meeting these basic expectations, and it starts to exceed a certain inconvenience or hassle threshold, the customer becomes a candidate for churn, ie defecting to the competition. Note that CRM can only favour retention, not guarantee it. The happiest customer using the best product with the most hassle-free customer service will not make one iota of difference if the customer feels like a change for whatever reason: the desire to try out something new, vendor image, to impress a partner, whatever. At the end of the day, CRM is not about ensuring your customer doesn't defect, but ensuring *you* don't provide the customer with a reason to do so.

Processes that favour increased profitability are those that: 1) recognize opportunities for increasing a customer's wallet share by cross-selling and up-selling; 2) are able to identify and target other customers or prospects with similar segmentation profiles. Such process improvement usually results from 'analytical CRM', which seeks to understand customer behaviour 'after the fact' by analysing the information aggregated from operational CRM systems and back-office systems.

CRM = reduced costs through better processes

Though no company ever saved its way to profitability, it is often overlooked that CRM can also generate very significant cost savings in the form of more effective (ie right) and more efficient (ie speedier) processes. After all, this was what BPR was all about, albeit without the technology and systems (see Chapter 1).

These reduced costs can usually be obtained in: 1) sales and marketing, through more cost-effective marketing campaigns and a shorter sales cycle; 2) order processing, where the staff required for order entry and verification can be drastically reduced, eg through the use of a product configurator that results in error-free orders.

In pharmaceutical companies, for example, around 15 per cent of revenue is spent on sales and marketing; for a billion-dollar company, that represents up to US $150 million. Even a crummy 1 per cent cost reduction through CRM process improvement would already generate US $1.5 million in savings. Real-world figures will clearly be much higher.

CRM FROM A CUSTOMER PERSPECTIVE

So much for CRM from a company perspective, but what about the customers' perspective? Customers of course don't view things in terms of CRM, which is a concept they've probably never heard of. They just see it as a company they'd rather be doing business with, for reasons they may or may not care to analyse, which can probably be summed up as 'a good product or service at the right price, and efficient and friendly service'.

Let's take two simple examples, one from business-to-consumer (personal banking) and one from business-to-business (telecommunications services).

Example 1 – personal banking

My earliest experience of CRM before the term was even invented was in banking in the mid-80s. Soon after I'd started working, I ended up with a current account, a savings account, a couple of tax-deductible insurance policies and a special home-loan account. Regardless of my increasing net worth each year, my current account was still subject to the same interest penalties the odd time I was in the red. The teller was only able to handle my current and savings accounts; I had to see two other people for the status of my insurance policies and home-loan account. And, not surprisingly, the bank was unable to give me a consolidated view of everything I had. Until I was considered rich enough to have a personal banker, I had to see each 'specialist teller' in turn, get the account statements and consolidate them myself. All I wanted from a 'CRM' perspective was to be able to talk to one person who had access to all my accounts, policies, investments etc, and be treated financially from the perspective of my net worth and potential for growth.

Fortunately, since then banks have evolved considerably in terms of processes and systems; any bank teller in front of a screen today has access to the basic status and balance information for most accounts. However, banks still have some way to go in being able to manage a customer from a net worth perspective, ie being able to send a consolidated statement of the sum of all different accounts, policies, investments, home loan or mortgage, shares etc, with this net worth determining interest rates.

Carrying on my CRM wish list for 2002, I wish I could do all of the above, plus other basic transactions – query my monthly account statement, be able to fix appointments etc – across the channel of my choice:

▮ At my local branch: in front of any teller and not just the person in charge of my accounts (except for cases when I need specialist advice, my so-called 'personal banker' adds no value compared to any other bank teller).

▮ Over the phone: to an anonymous call-centre agent (I'd only need to talk to my personal banker if I wanted specialist advice).

▮ On the Web: on a special 'My Accounts' screen that gives me a heads-up of all my accounts after entering my customer ID, without me having to type in half a dozen account numbers. If I had an issue with anything I was looking at, I should be able to click a 'call me now' button to talk to a call-centre agent.

And, of course, there has to be coherency across channels, if not real-time then at least on a next-day basis. So if I fix an appointment on the Web, I want to be able to call up the next day and be able to change it. If I carry out a funds transfer over the phone, I want to be able to see that on the Web the next time I log on.

And finally, as the cherry on the cake, I'd like to be able to define alerts (eg an account balance that drops below a certain amount), which would generate a message on my mobile phone, or an e-mail. Any bank that could provide all of the above would have me as a long-term customer with no desire to go elsewhere. If I did switch, it would be for reasons beyond their control.

Example 2 – B-to-B telecommunications

Acme Nuts and Bolts is an SME (small or medium enterprise), with a main office in the city and a production facility 20 minutes away on the outskirts. It uses a combined telephone and Internet 'bundle' from a newly established telco, with long-distance and international calling plus basic Internet access for its two sites.

Though the bundled product offering is reasonably priced and reliable, the ongoing relationship in terms of service and enquiries is far from satisfactory. Acme would like a consolidated monthly invoice for telephone and Internet services. Instead, it has to deal with separate invoices, each in a different format and each with a different customer number. Similarly, Acme would like to call a single number for enquiries. Instead, it has to call two different numbers, each with a very different quality of service. Most frustratingly, the Internet service desk has no visibility on anything from the telephone side, and vice versa. In fact, the Internet service desk doesn't even know that Acme is also a customer for telephone services.

The main gripe Acme has is the impression it is dealing with two different vendors, one for telephone services and another for the Internet, each with its own quality of service, and neither aware that Acme uses a combined telephone/Internet bundle. Only the monthly billing shows this.

What Acme doesn't know is that behind the scenes it really *is* dealing with two different vendors: the telephone part of the business acquired the Internet side two years ago, but the two have never merged organizationally. The bundle is a commercial product offering from the parent company, which is basically a discount for taking both telephone and Internet service. Apart from this discount, it would have exactly the same level of service if it had signed two separate contracts with each part of the company.

Since Acme is satisfied with the price and the overall reliability of the service, its 'CRM wish list' is really very simple: to be able to deal with a single company in terms of billing, service and enquiries, with a single telephone number and a single point of contact aware of all service issues and customer interactions, regardless of whether it concerns the telephone or the Internet. This would reduce the administrative burden for Acme when dealing with its telco.

If a competitor came along that was able to meet this requirement, and offered a better deal financially, Acme would be a good candidate for defection, especially since the costs and inconvenience of installing and setting up this type of service are minimal.

CRM FROM A SYSTEMS PERSPECTIVE

We've seen CRM from a company and a customer perspective. Let us now take a look at systems. Figure 2.6 shows CRM from a systems perspective, applied to the simplified three-stage customer life cycle.

At one end of the spectrum (top of Figure 2.6), we have those famous islands of automation, ie different systems built for different functions at different times, with little or no design relationships between them and of course no interfaces. As each system has

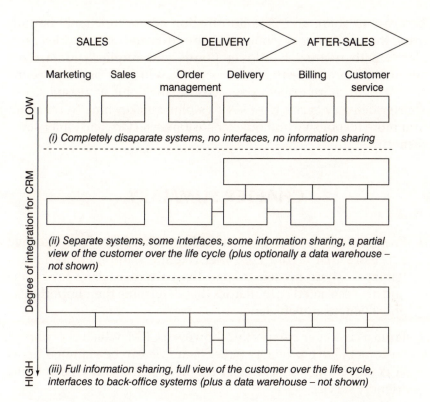

Figure 2.6 *CRM from a systems perspective (main systems shown)*

its own customer database and its own data model, any information collected upstream has to be rekeyed downstream, from marketing through sales, delivery and after-sales.

At the other end of the spectrum (bottom of Figure 2.6), there exists the ideal world of a single system spanning all functions across the customer life cycle. With multiple applications accessing a single customer database, there is no duplication of data and consequently no need for any interfaces. There is real-time flow-through of: 1) leads from marketing to sales; 2) orders from sales to delivery; 3) customer and order information to customer service. Of course, this is virtually impossible, even for start-ups (see page 59), but it helps to position the target for CRM.

Between the two we can have various degrees of commonality and interfaces, dependent on how the information system in the enterprise has evolved over time (middle of Figure 2.6). The closer we get to the ideal end of the spectrum, the more possible it becomes to share and pass information across functional boundaries, thus reducing or eliminating the costs and complexities associated with manual handover points and duplicate data. This results in more cost-effective processes, which in business terms translates to shorter sales cycles (cost savings plus increased sales), shorter delivery cycles (cost savings plus quicker time to revenue) and more responsive and quicker customer service (customer satisfaction).

CHAPTER SUMMARY

▌ From a company perspective, CRM can be defined as 'effective processes that favour customer retention and increased profitability'. These processes span the customer-facing functions, and are associated with metrics that determine their importance, effectiveness and efficiency.

▌ From a customer perspective, however, CRM, which is a concept customers have probably never heard of, can be summed up as 'a good product or service at the right price, and efficient and friendly service'.

▌ From a systems perspective, CRM is about sharing and passing information between systems across functional boundaries, enabling an enterprise-wide view of the customer, and reducing the costs and complexities associated with manual handover points and duplicate data.

Part II

Critical success factors for CRM

3

Organizational readiness for CRM

Systems tend to resemble the organizations that build them.
(Conway's Law)

One of the biggest myths about CRM is thinking that any company can embrace it and expect results. Well, that's like thinking anyone can run the New York Marathon. Depending on your physical readiness (in terms of weight, training and endurance), you could be months or years away from even entering, let alone completing the race. Similarly, a minimum 'organizational readiness rating' (in terms of customer, process and systems maturity) must be in place for CRM to happen.

SHOULD YOU EVEN BE LOOKING AT CRM?

Since CRM is about identifying, retaining and increasing the profitability of your best customers, something every business under the sun ultimately wants to do, it seems the last question you'd want to ask is whether CRM is for you. Unfortunately, because you have only a one in five chance of success, and simply attempting the feat will set you back anything between US $5,000 and US $15,000 per user per year, you certainly want to be very sure you can answer this question.

As a rule of thumb, you should be looking at CRM if you can answer yes to as many of the following questions as possible, which were consolidated from two sources: 1) René Lefébure and Gilles Venturi (2001) in their book *Gestion de la Relation Client* [Customer Relationship Management]; 2) Geoffrey Ables in discussion thread 107 on www.crmguru.com entitled 'Do we really need a CRM system yet?'

▌ Do you have a large number of people in sales and service in direct contact with customers, say more than 30?

▌ Are you in a highly collaborative environment, with customer interaction requiring input from multiple players within each function (sales and service)?

▌ Do you sell complex products that require a high degree of configuration and customization?

▌ Do you have a large number of customers, say more than 10,000?

▌ Is a typical customer relationship worth a lot to you from a profit standpoint, ie will it cost you to lose one?

▌ Can your customers interact with you across multiple channels?

▌ Do you have frequent contact with large groups of customers, or all customers, across multiple channels?

▌ Is there a need to customize what you are saying to each customer through these channels?

If you have answered yes to a lot of these questions, then you can consider yourself a candidate for CRM. If not, then the costs and organizational disruption that CRM entails would not be worth the benefits, and you should look to simpler tools like contact managers to address those business processes (see Figure 2.4) that need fixing.

CUSTOMER MATURITY

The quote at the beginning of Chapter 2 ('If a company lost 10 per cent of its inventory, it would react very quickly. But if it lost 10 per cent of its customers to the competition, it probably wouldn't even be aware of it'.) is a litmus test of whether a company's operations revolve around the products or services it sells, or around its customers.

The vast majority of companies would fail the above test. As for those that would pass, the chances are: 1) the customer has long been gone and it's too late to do anything about it; 2) there is little or no information in electronic format that can be analysed to try to understand why the customer left, eg customer service interactions, information on product usage or billing patterns.

Most companies have a very good idea of what it costs to build and ship a product, or create a new service, and the overall revenue generated (they'd have to, if only to be able to calculate their margins). And while most companies can break down their revenue by product, there are some that can't do even this, ie they are only able to see the final figures for all products combined. For example, some telcos can only see the total network usage for all products combined, and are unable to tell which products generate the most billing.

However, things start to get murky when it comes to the customer side, mainly:

▌ Who is likely to buy a given product or service? The answer would enable us to target prospects with a similar profile and convert them to customers.

▌ Why do customers leave for the competition? The answers would enable us to fix the associated problems, and to identify those customers facing similar issues and possibly prevent them from leaving as well.

▌ How do customers actually use a product or service, and what is the nature of their interactions with the company? The answers would enable us to identify opportunities for cross-selling and up-selling.

Customer maturity is therefore a measure of how far a company has evolved from a product-based operational model (ie moving products out of the door at minimum cost) to a customer-based operational model (ie 'Who's buying our products, why do they like us, how can we measure satisfaction, why do they leave and how can we sell them more?'). The most important measurement of customer maturity is the existence of a unique customer identifier across multiple systems.

Some examples of customer maturity in practical terms would be task forces or projects with the objective of better understanding the customer, for example:

▮ benchmarking certain processes with respect to the competition;

▮ talking to real customers;

▮ trying to identify one's most profitable customers;

▮ talking to ex-customers to try to understand why they left;

▮ quickly answering customers' most frequently asked questions.

Most of the above are stepping stones to CRM, and could result in one or more of the following systems deliverables:

▮ a data warehouse, or one or more data marts (optionally with data mining capabilities);

▮ a sales force automation (SFA) system;

▮ a marketing information system;

▮ a one-stop-shop call centre for all customer enquiries; etc.

Each of the above evolutionary steps can take anything from six months to two years or more – and cost millions of dollars in the process. The higher the level of customer maturity, therefore, the lower will be the barriers on the road to CRM.

PROCESS MATURITY

Process maturity can best be summed up by the following sayings: 1) 'If you don't know where you are, a map won't help'; 2) 'You can't improve what you can't measure'. In other words, the ease with which CRM tools and technology can be absorbed into the enterprise is directly dependent on how mature the processes are across the customer-facing functions of sales, marketing and customer service.

Instead of trying to build a process maturity model for sales, marketing and customer service, let us fall back on a simple analogy from the field of software development or software engineering. Building on the comparison between CASE and CRM (see Chapter

1), it became readily apparent that the ability for an IT organization to absorb CASE tools and technology was directly dependent on the IT department's process maturity. This led to the famous (at least in IT circles) 'Process Maturity Levels' defined by Watts Humphrey of the Software Engineering Institute (SEI) in 1989 in his ground-breaking book, *Managing the Software Process*, reproduced below from an article in *iSeries NEWS* of April 1993:

- Level 1: *Initial*. Until the process is under statistical control, orderly progress in process improvement is not possible. While there are many degrees of statistical control, the first step is to achieve rudimentary predictability of schedules and costs.
- Level 2: *Repeatable*. The organisation has achieved a stable process with a repeatable level of statistical control by initiating rigorous project management of commitments, costs, schedules, and changes.
- Level 3: *Defined*. The organisation has defined the process as a basis for consistent implementation and better understanding. At this point, advanced technology can usefully be introduced.
- Level 4: *Managed*. The organisation now has a foundation for continuing improvement and optimisation of the process.

Read T Fleming put it in more conversational English with his 'Five Ages of Methodology Sophistication' (reproduced from the same article in *iSeries NEWS* of April 1993):

- *The Age of Anarchy:* Anything goes.
- *The Age of Folklore:* Wisdom is passed from one generation of engineers to another, over beer and pizza.
- *The Age of Methodology:* The way software is to be engineered is documented, and it is actually done that way.
- *The Age of Metrics:* Both the products and the processes are measured in standardised ways.
- *The Age of Enlightenment:* Productivity is achieved through continuous quality improvement, much as it is done in manufacturing.

It doesn't take much imagination to see that the above maturity levels could apply equally well to a company's processes like sales, marketing and customer service, eg for sales simply replace the words 'the software development process' with 'the selling process', and 'engineers' with 'sales reps'.

Customer service and order management departments are by definition more process-oriented, because of the task- and measurement-oriented nature of their work, ie delivering orders and handling customer enquiries (whether their processes are effective, though, is another subject altogether).

Sales and marketing, however, are notorious for their lack of process, because of the non-mechanistic nature of their work. It is routine for marketing, for example, to have little or no idea of campaign effectiveness. As for sales reps, they are by definition individualistic and averse to rules – what counts is closing the deal; the how is secondary. Even the sales funnel, that instrument that was supposed to introduce a minimum of process and measurement, is generally viewed by the sales rep as a reporting nuisance more than anything else: between first contact with a prospect and the closing of a deal, black magic is alive and well! There is therefore an enormous window of opportunity to improve processes in sales and marketing.

Some examples of process maturity in practical terms are task forces or projects with the objective of improving the metrics shown in Figure 2.5:

- lead close ratios;

- sales cycle duration;

- delivery cycle time;

- first-call resolution rate;

- etc.

Such metrics are inextricably linked to CRM, and could result in one or more of the following systems deliverables:

- an SFA system;

- an order configurator;

- call-centre software and an automatic call distributor (ACD);

- interfaces between systems to eliminate the rekeying of information and speed up throughput;

- etc.

In practice, then, companies not yet at the 'repeatable' stage will find it extremely difficult, if not impossible, to implement CRM software, for the simple reason that there are no processes to automate! Instead of jumping into the deep end of CRM, they should instead concentrate on defining their basic processes. These can then be gradually automated with the help of simple tools like contact managers. Typically, such companies would include start-ups (see page 59).

Just as for customer maturity (above), each of the above process maturity steps can take anything from six months to two years or more – and cost millions of dollars in the process. The higher the level of process maturity from 'repeatable' upwards, the lower will be the barriers on the road to CRM.

SYSTEMS MATURITY

As a function of the customer and process maturity initiatives discussed above, we will begin to see an evolution in systems maturity: 1) transactional systems evolve from 'islands of automation' to interfaced systems (see Figure 3.1, which is essentially Figure 2.6

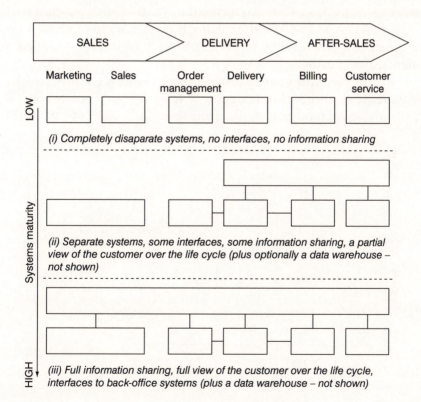

Figure 3.1 *Systems maturity (transactional systems)*

with a different vertical scale); 2) decision support becomes part of the landscape, with transactional systems consolidated to form a data warehouse, and optionally data marts (see Figure 3.2).

The growth in systems maturity is a long-term process, with key interfaces and a data warehouse taking anything from six months to two years or more. The higher the level of systems maturity therefore, the lower will be the barriers on the road to CRM.

PEOPLE AND MOTIVATIONAL MATURITY

Last but not least, let's not forget about people, without whom no processes and systems are going to work anyway. People are not going to embrace CRM spontaneously; they have to be motivated to do so.

Figure 3.3 shows the famous Maslow triangle, widely known to all students of psychology and to anyone who has studied the basics of motivation. First put forward by motivational psychologist Andrew Maslow in 1943, it explains how motivation is based on personal and environmental prerequisites, which Maslow called a 'hierarchy of needs'.

For example, you cannot ask people to embrace concepts like achievement and status (esteem) if they haven't got the basic prerequisites of food and shelter (physiological). Similarly, it would

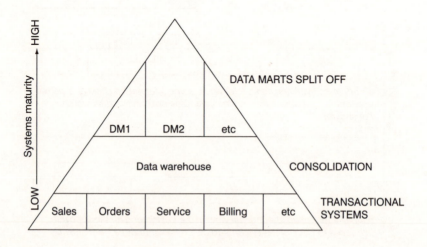

Figure 3.2 *Systems maturity (decision support)*

Figure 3.3 *Maslow's 'hierarchy of needs' triangle*

be a mistake to assume that people will be naturally motivated to embrace CRM because it makes sense and is good for the customer, the company, etc. Certain personal and environmental prerequisites will also therefore apply.

Drawing on Maslow's approach, we can put together a 'hierarchy of needs' for people to be motivated to embrace CRM. Now, before I get taken to pieces by psychologists and other specialists for getting in way over my head on a subject like motivation for which I'm patently not qualified, let me stress that it is only the 'hierarchy of needs' *analogy* I'm interested in. If someone wants to go and research the subject further and put different needs in the triangle, that's fine by me. At the humble level of this book, all I'm suggesting are common-sense needs to get across the point that users need to have a reason to be motivated for CRM.

With that qualifier out of the way, let's now look at the CRM 'hierarchy of needs' triangle in Figure 3.4. What this is essentially saying is that people will be more likely to be motivated to take up CRM if their job description is relevant to it. This would then be made even easier if they are generally satisfied with their careers, and benefit from a good working environment and don't have to worry about losing their jobs.

Conversely, it will be difficult to motivate people to embrace CRM if their job descriptions have little to do with it. This is then further compounded if they are earning the minimum wage and doing what they perceive as unchallenging work. Throw in a poor

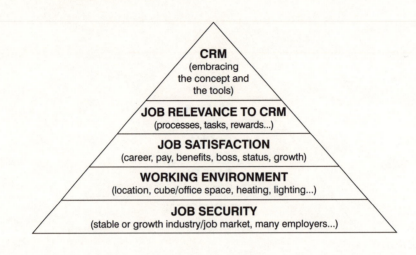

Figure 3.4 *CRM 'hierarchy of needs' triangle*

working environment with a high turnover and the possibility of lay-offs, eg as in a recession, and it gets even worse.

In practice, issues surrounding CRM motivation usually kick in at the job satisfaction and job relevance levels, eg by bolting on CRM responsibilities to existing jobs without redefining performance and pay. The first people who usually come to mind are call-centre agents, whose performance criteria are rarely linked to real customer satisfaction but to throughput based on Tayloristic tasks with little intellectual challenge (Taylor was the founder of so-called time and motion studies at the beginning of the 20th century). In the caricatured but alas far from uncommon scenario, a company will spend millions of dollars implementing a CRM system and then put it in front of call-centre agents on the minimum wage whose performance criteria are based on call quantity rather than quality. Another example is in sales, where it is difficult to get top-performing salespeople to buy into CRM when they associate it with deskilling their jobs and helping their manager to look over their shoulder and give away the best bits of their territory to others.

In conclusion, it's not sufficient for a company at executive level to buy into CRM and then preach the gospel to the rest of the people and expect them to embrace it too. People will only buy into CRM when it has relevance to their jobs and is rewarded as such, ie when they are motivated to do so and when they've been properly trained to feel comfortable with it.

DEBUNKING THE START-UP MYTH

Given the difficulties of implementing CRM in established companies with their entrenched processes, people and systems, it would be tempting to think that start-ups represent the potential for CRM nirvana. Certainly that would seem a logical conclusion to draw, since start-ups are not burdened with legacy systems, and have the energy and the opportunity to get it right from the beginning.

For example, during a presentation I attended at a CRM vendor–user group conference in 2001, a VP from an international telco put up a slide entitled 'It's easy for newcomers/start-ups!', with the basic message that they had the luxury of implementing an out-of-the-box solution with no integration issues. Unfortunately, reality shows otherwise: trying to implement CRM in a start-up environment can actually be more difficult than in established companies – for a whole different set of reasons (see Chapter 13, Case study 2).

We can define a start-up as any operation (parent company or subsidiary) in business for less than two years, experiencing double- or triple-digit annual growth, with staff doubling each year. Here's what you can expect to find on your first visit:

▌ Whatever function you're looking at – sales, customer service, finance, HR – there are not enough people. With everyone overworked – with their own job plus usually someone else's as well – it's extremely difficult to get commitment from people even to come to a meeting.

▌ At least one or two of the key executive positions in marketing, sales, order management and customer service are either not yet filled, or TBH (to be hired), or acting. When such positions are filled, the incumbent has a half-life of around 6–12 months, by which time he or she either resigns, gets fired or gets promoted, whichever comes first. So any executive sponsorship or commitment is ultimately precarious.

▌ Sales reps are out prospecting and selling all the time, using a combination of manual methods, Excel, Access, Filemaker Pro etc and various contact managers on a purely individual basis. And all this information needs ultimately to find its way into the future CRM system.

■ Process maturity is very low or non-existent. What processes do end up taking shape are rarely the direct result of any high-level thought on the subject, but simply a combination of expediency and the work methods of those who set up the department.

■ When there is an IT manager or director, that person's main role is to manage the logistics of PCs for new arrivals, have a functioning help desk, ensure adequate bandwidth on the LAN and deal with MAN/WAN connections to remote sites or regional headquarters or the parent company. CRM is not even on the radar screen, which is just as well because it would make the IT manager or director's already stressful life a whole lot worse.

In short, all heads are focused on revenue growth with limited resources, which is the criterion by which the CEO will be measured and that the stock market will reward. Acquisition is the name of the game – everything else is secondary – including retention and CRM (which any start-up will understandably deny with much vehemence). In such an environment, with low process maturity, organizational instability and insufficient people, CRM stands first and foremost for disruption.

And when, as is often the case, the CRM initiative originates from the parent company as part of a global project, the start-up subsidiaries will pay due lip-service to the importance of the project, but a week after the kick-off all those well-intentioned commitments fly right out of the window, things get back to 'normal' and the project stalls.

The firm recommendation for anyone even contemplating CRM in a start-up environment is to wait until the organization has reached a minimum level of maturity in terms of processes and people. In the meantime, just give them a contact manager (see page 50).

THE ORGANIZATIONAL READINESS RATING

This chapter can be summarized into an organizational readiness rating, which is a measure of how mature an organization is for CRM (see Table 3.1). Like all surveys, analyses and questionnaires, the final score categories are fairly broad. Their objective is to make you think about your own situation overall and not to pigeon-hole you into a given category based on mathematical precision.

Table 3.1 *Organizational readiness rating*

CRITERIA	ANSWERS	SCORE
1 Should you even be looking at CRM? – Do you have a large number of people in sales and service in direct contact with customers? – Are you in a highly collaborative environment, with customer interaction requiring input from multiple players across different functions (sales and service)? – Do you sell complex products that require a high degree of configuration and customization? – Do you have a large number of customers? – Is a typical customer relationship worth a lot to you from a profit standpoint, ie will it cost you to lose one? – Can your customers interact with you across multiple channels? – Do you have frequent contact with large groups of customers, or all customers, across multiple channels? – Is there a need to customize what you are saying to each customer through these channels?	– If number of YES answers is three or less, then you are not a likely candidate for CRM. You should instead consider using simple tools like contact managers to address those business processes that need fixing. – If number of YES answers is four or more, then score 1 point for this question and continue.	
2 Customer maturity: Is there a unique customer identifier (real or cross-referenced) across at least two of the following system categories: sales, order management, billing, customer service?	YES = 2 NO = 0 Use as score.	
3 Process maturity: Are you at a maturity level of at least 2 (ie 'repeatable', see page 53) in the following functional areas? – Marketing (YES = 2, NO = 0) – Sales (YES = 3, NO = 0) – Order management (YES = 1, NO = 0) – Billing (YES = 1, NO = 0) – Customer service (YES = 1, NO = 0)	Add up answers and use total as score	
4 Systems maturity: – Do you have a data warehouse that consolidates customers and products? (YES = 3) – Do you have an automatic interface between sales and order management, ie no double entry? (YES = 2)	Add up answers and use total as score	

Table 3.1 *continued*

CRITERIA	ANSWERS	SCORE
– Do you have an automatic interface (ie no double entry) between customer service and at least one of the following: sales, order management, billing? (YES = 2)		
5 People and motivational maturity: Would you say that your people are sufficiently motivated to embrace CRM concepts and tools because it is generally relevant to their current jobs?	YES = 3 NO = 0 Use as score	
6 Is your company in start-up mode, ie in existence for two years or less? Even if your parent company is no longer a start-up, do you have multiple subsidiaries you are considering for CRM that are in start-up mode?	YES = –5 (subtract!) NO = 0	
TOTAL =>		

SCORE	CONCLUSION
7 or less	Your company is not yet ready for CRM, because of a low organizational maturity in terms of customers, processes and systems. It would be more beneficial to concentrate on process improvement, possibly with the help of simple tools like contact managers.
8–14	Your company is ready for CRM, because of an acceptable level of organizational maturity in terms of customers, processes and systems. However, this maturity is only at an intermediate stage, which means that a lot of work still needs to be done (ie one to three years) before a CRM project starts to yield tangible benefits.
15–21	A rare occurrence, your company is ready for CRM because of a sufficiently high level of organizational maturity in terms of customers, processes, systems – and even people. You should be able to embrace CRM concepts and tools relatively quickly, as these are a logical extension of the evolution of your organization to date. You can expect tangible benefits in as little as one to two years.

Based on the results, you should decide:

▌ not to proceed at all with CRM, and seek alternative solutions; or

▌ to proceed with caution, ie don't expect tangible results before two to three years; or

▌ to proceed with reasonable optimism, ie you can expect tangible results in one to two years.

The main conclusion is that, while CRM can indeed be for everyone, there are many prerequisites that usually take a few years to achieve. In short, ensure your company first learns to walk before it attempts to run.

CHAPTER SUMMARY

▮ Depending on certain factors (number of customers, number of people in contact with them, average value of a customer relationship etc) it is entirely possible that your organization is not a candidate for CRM, and can get by with simpler tools like contact managers to improve key processes.

▮ The term 'organizational readiness' refers to the ability of a company to absorb CRM into its operations based on its level of maturity in terms of customers, processes and systems. The higher the maturity level of each component, the lower will be the barriers on the road to CRM.

▮ Customer maturity is a measure of how far a company has evolved from a product-based operational model to a customer-based operational model, and can take anything from six months to two years or more to achieve. The most important measurement of customer maturity is the existence of a unique customer identifier across multiple systems.

▮ Process maturity is a measure of how far a company's processes have evolved from 'the age of anarchy' to 'the age of metrics', and can take anything from six months to two years or more to achieve. The most important measurement of process maturity is the ability to achieve 'repeatable' predictability of schedules, costs and commitments, which lays the foundations for process improvement through CRM.

▮ Systems maturity is a measure of how far a company's systems have evolved to reflect the company's level of customer and process maturity. The most important measurement of systems maturity is the evolution from 'islands of automation' to interfaced systems that share and pass information across functional boundaries.

▮ People or motivational maturity is a measure of the ability of employees to embrace CRM from the perspective of job relevance and job satisfaction. The most important measurement of motivational maturity is when CRM is part and parcel of people's job descriptions in terms of pay and performance.

▌ The relatively low level of customer, process and systems maturity in start-ups makes them poor candidates for CRM. In such an environment, with the focus on revenue growth, CRM stands first and foremost for disruption. Until the organization has reached a minimum level of maturity, automation should be limited to basic systems like a contact manager.

4

A valid business case, with measurable benefits

Not all things that can be counted count, and not all things that count can be counted.

(Albert Einstein)

THE BUSINESS CASE

A CRM project should have a valid business case, ie a recognized and identifiable business problem to solve, and measurable benefits to justify the investment. Some examples are:

▌ Decrease customer churn by x per cent, which should increase revenue by so many millions.

▌ Shorten the sales cycle for product ABC to three weeks, which should increase sales by at least x per cent.

▌ Reduce delivery cycle for product XYZ from three weeks to five days, which should eliminate post-order customer defection and generate so many millions more in reduced time to revenue.

▌ Answer 80 per cent of customer enquiries immediately, and the remaining 20 per cent within three working days. Quarterly customer satisfaction ratings to increase from 30 per cent to at least 80 per cent.

▌ Increase cross-selling and/or up-selling by x per cent or so many millions.

You can even go as far as saying that, unless your business case starts with the word 'increase' or 'decrease', and you can write it on the back of a business card or explain it in a five-second soundbite, you don't have a business case. All the lofty-sounding and overused business cases like '100 per cent customer satisfaction', 'one world, one view', 'cradle to grave', 'customer journey' etc cannot be measured and are therefore ultimately unconvincing (any reference to actual projects is entirely coincidental).

It could be argued that, since CRM is by nature strategic, cross-functional and all-embracing, it cannot be reduced to the back of a business card or a soundbite. Nor are business benefits so easy to measure. From a discussion or a philosophical point of view, that might be true. From a nuts-and-bolts project perspective, however, ie when talking resources, deliverables and risk, it ultimately has to be broken down into one or more discrete tactical components (and the fewer the better). If you can't do this, then the project is too wide in scope and should be scaled back (see Chapter 6).

Or using the familiar SMART acronym, a business case should be:

▌ S – specific;

▌ M – measurable;

▌ A – actionable;

▌ R – realistic;

▌ T – timely.

By these criteria, it should come as no surprise that many CRM projects don't have a valid business case. Not only that, they are usually IT-initiated and IT-driven, resulting in a project with a technology focus rather than a business focus.

MEASURING BENEFITS FOR ROI

For those projects that potentially do have a business case, the expected benefits are usually insufficiently quantified. Though these benefits may be clear to some people, eg the project team and especially the end users, they have to be officially measured against unambiguous, pre-project metrics. And that's the crux of the matter: the high costs of CRM projects and the inevitable requirement for additional funding later on mean that the bean counters will naturally ask for proof of ROI. And in the absence of a documented before/after picture, any numbers presented after implementation are inevitably viewed as suspect.

Yet for all this emphasis on pre-project measurement, the plain truth is that it's not that easy. Unless a company is already at a certain level of process maturity (see Chapter 3), there are usually no baseline data available. CRM also results in intangible or soft benefits that are hard to quantify, eg employee motivation or customer referrals. Yet this should not be an excuse to move forward only on faith: it is always possible to measure something, which is preferable to measuring nothing at all. Any company that puts its mind to it can, within a few weeks, come up with some measurements that can be used for before and after comparisons. Here are three examples:

∎ If you ask a CRM-aware person (a consultant or a member of the project team) to shadow a sales rep, a sales manager or a customer service rep for a week, you will definitely discover a wealth of measurable information concerning leads, opportunities, orders, trouble tickets etc.

∎ You could analyse your current processes in a one- or two-day workshop session as part of a cross-functional team. This needs to be carefully managed though, because such sessions naturally flow over into process improvement sessions (it is a good thing to capture process improvement ideas while people's creative juices are flowing, but it is essential not to lose sight of the main objective of the workshop, which is to understand the current situation).

∎ Though much more complex and probably not doable inside of a few weeks – especially for companies at a low level of process maturity – it would also be extremely beneficial to get a 'before snapshot' of indicators of customer retention and loyalty. This would be applicable in medium-/high-frequency repeat-business environments, ie business-to-consumer (B-to-C), but also in some business-to-business (B-to-B) sectors serving the SME and small office, home office (SOHO) market segments. Such indicators would rely on behaviour-based modelling, which helps to predict repeat purchasing, which in turn drives customer value. An example is the basic but effective RFM model: R – recency ('How recently has the customer interacted with us?'), F – frequency ('How often does the customer interact with us?'), M – monetary ('How much has the customer purchased to date?'). The model then allows us to assign 'scores' for all customers, directly related to their value. A successful CRM project should see a positive change in customer value over time. (See www.jimnovo.com for more information on this subject.)

Now just because you're reduced to this type of fishing for before/after metrics doesn't mean you don't have a legitimate business case; it simply means you're trying to wrap some numbers around your current processes – probably for the very first time. I have seen a number of CRM projects that, though inevitably expensive, nonetheless delivered a clear and undisputable ROI many times over, and were recognized by the business users as doing so. However, the executive sponsor soon moved on, and there were no official baseline metrics against which to measure these post-implementation benefits. So instead of being lauded and applauded, the project team, though duly recognized, still had to row against the tide to 'prove' the success of the project and get the funding needed for phase two.

This cannot be stressed enough: take the time to formalize the current situation and the associated metrics. When the executive sponsor is no longer around, it's the only official leg you'll have to stand on. It's therefore one of the best investments you can make before implementing a new system.

CHAPTER SUMMARY

▌ Ensure you have a business case that is unambiguous and easily understandable, addresses a clearly identifiable business problem and can yield measurable benefits.

∎ Define the key before/after metrics that will be used to measure these benefits, and how soon after the implementation (both pilot and roll-out) the comparison will be made; otherwise no ROI can be measured.

∎ During the project, constantly reassess the allocation of resources to ensure that the most important benefits are achieved and the users acknowledge them.

5

A credible and active executive sponsor

The difference between involvement and commitment? When you have bacon and eggs for breakfast, the hen is involved, but the pig is committed.
(John A Price, quoted in MacHale, 1997)

If there's at least one critical success factor that comes as no surprise and is agreed by all, it is the requirement for a CRM project to have an executive sponsor to sell the business case and drive the project. However, it's not sufficient to have an executive's name associated with a project for credibility; there's much more to it than that.

INVOLVEMENT OR COMMITMENT

In most cases, executive sponsors are sold on CRM either by consultants or by a departmental director over lunch or during a meeting. Most of the initial legwork is therefore done by others. Executive sponsors then come to the project launch meeting to set the scene and stress the importance of the project for the company, do the obligatory 10-minute introduction – and then hand over to a director or manager and leave for another meeting. Usually you don't see much of them afterwards, and they go back to the hundred and one other things that VPs usually do. Now just because sponsors signed for the budget doesn't necessarily mean they are accountable for the project at board level. VPs approve lots of big-ticket budgets, but that doesn't necessarily mean that they get on the agenda for board meetings or that the CEO even gets to hear about them.

From there onwards, executive sponsors become figureheads whose distance from the day-to-day running of the project creates a host of problems for the project manager. This mainly concerns lack of business input from middle management, and a lack of direction on key organizational issues that can only be resolved at VP level. This is not surprising, since the business usually sees CRM as being primarily about systems and technology, which explains why sponsors are quite content to turn over the running of the project to others, usually IT.

WILL THE REAL EXECUTIVE SPONSOR PLEASE STAND UP?

Since CRM is a business project, with business issues to resolve, *real* executive sponsors would correspond to the following criteria:

▌ They initiated the project, or were convinced by one or more direct reports over a sufficiently long period of time (months, rather than days) for there to have been some information gathering, strategic consulting, research, benchmarking etc. Sponsors at this stage are usually able to stand up and defend the project to either the board or the CEO.

▌ They will be accountable for the project, which becomes part of their objectives.

▌ With clear responsibility and accountability, but also very much aware that they won't have the time to play an active role, they assign or recruit a dedicated resource for the job. Usually a director or manager, this person is the project 'owner', who not only represents the sponsor but, probably more important, actually runs the project on a day-to-day basis, usually in partnership with the IT project or programme manager.

WHY THE CEO SHOULD NOT BE THE EXECUTIVE SPONSOR

Now who should this sponsor be? There is a school of thought that holds that the best, if not the only credible, executive sponsor for CRM is the CEO. At first glance, this makes a lot of sense; after all, you can't go any higher, and the CEO represents the whole enterprise, cutting across functions, departments, politics and turf.

Alas, reality is different. Last time I checked, the role of the CEO was to run the company. To do this he or she deals with strategy and makes key decisions. The rest is details, and details are delegated, firstly to the board, which then delegates in turn at its level. Being an executive sponsor for a CRM project in the sense of responsibility and accountability is not, never has been and never will be a role for a CEO. If you want to stand in the shortest line, go and stand behind the CEO who is a real, as opposed to a figurehead, exec sponsor for CRM in the company. Rightly or wrongly, in the vast majority of companies, as far as the CEO is concerned, CRM might as well stand for 'Can't Really Matter'.

For the person running the company, any other responsibility is necessarily secondary, and therefore not credible. Can you imagine Bill Gates being the executive sponsor for CRM at Microsoft? (I know I should be saying Steve Ballmer, but the impact isn't the same.) It might look pretty impressive for an outsider, but if I were working at Microsoft, a CRM project sponsored by Bill Gates would ultimately be a CRM project not sponsored by anyone. It's a bit like those e-mails sent by the CEO to the 'All employees @' address warning people that they have one week to update their personal details in a so-called company-wide directory that is used by all of 10 people at corporate headquarters (the remaining 20,000 employees use the global directory in Outlook or cc:Mail). When the CEO endorses such initiatives, most people hit the delete button right away.

In summary, all a CEO can ever be for a CRM project is a strategic thinker, a banker, an arbitrator and a motivator – and even this will usually be a rare occurrence. Assuming you find the exceptional CEO who actually understands the importance of transforming the company via CRM *and* wants to do something about it, he or she would naturally have to assign it to a very high-level executive, perhaps a board member or even a newly created post. This person would then have a mandate for change that would result in the re-engineering of the functions and fiefdoms of all of the direct reports to the CEO. Well, I'm sure that the board members would wish this person well, and go out of their way to ensure he or she gets all the cooperation needed to ensure the project meets with a resounding success...

A REPRESENTATIVE STEERING COMMITTEE

The reality of organizational politics means that the executive sponsor stands every chance of being one of the existing senior executives, usually in sales, marketing or operations (customer service executives rarely start CRM projects).

Even with the right executive sponsor (accountability) and project owner (responsibility) identified, it is also important to have sponsorship from each functional executive who will be affected. I would recommend at least sales and marketing, and probably service as well. Some middle managers will choose to deprioritize the project if their boss is not publicly committed. The executive sponsor should therefore preside over a cross-functional steering committee of at least sales, marketing and IT directors. This avoids the perception that it is a project owned by any one function that is being imposed on the others.

CHAPTER SUMMARY

▌ Ensure you have a credible and active executive sponsor, ie one who is responsible and accountable for the project, and able to stand up and defend it to either the board or the CEO.

▌ The executive sponsor cannot and should not be the CEO. In the unlikely event of actually getting the CEO's heart and mind for CRM, he or she should remain a combination of strategic thinker, banker, arbitrator and motivator. But the CEO's name should *not* be associated with the project; otherwise it is no longer credible.

▌ Since executive sponsors already have their hands full with their normal jobs, the only way they can live up to their role is to assign or recruit a director or manager (the project owner) to run the project on a day-to-day basis, in direct relation with the IT project or programme manager.

▌ To avoid the perception that the project is owned by one function and is being imposed on the others, the executive sponsor should preside over a steering committee of at least the sales, marketing and IT directors, and if possible the customer service director.

6

A realistic project scope

I can believe anything, as long as it's incredible.
(Oscar Wilde, quoted in MacHale, 1997)

CRM AS A JOURNEY, NOT A DESTINATION

CRM spans many functions and promises many benefits. Those considering CRM may feel like the mouse in the maze containing small morsels of every conceivable kind of cheese, mentioned in the first paragraph of Chapter 1. It is only natural to want to share the benefits with as much of the enterprise as possible. The tendency is therefore strong to want to deliver results across multiple functions for day one, or very soon after.

But even a mouse can only eat so much cheese before it gets overwhelmed and can take no more. And so it is at project level: there are only so many benefits you can try to deliver before you get overwhelmed too.

One would have thought that, after the trials and tribulations of the ERP era just past, with the painful memories of big-bang implementations across multiple functions still fresh in our minds, we would proceed cautiously with CRM. Our pioneering ERP forebears had little choice in the matter, but with CRM we at least have the luxury of avoiding the big bang and proceeding in phases, one function at a time. But do we? Alas, no!

The vision is so enticing (or the business demands too much too soon) that we end up planning for day one deliverables that are so ambitious that we should by rights end up in the CRM hall of fame after implementation. How ambitious? Well, let me count the ways:

■ Move the whole sales force to a new sales automation tool, replacing islands of automation like Excel, Access and Filemaker Pro.

■ Have marketing use a new lead generation module, fully integrated with the sales automation tool, which will allow them to pass leads to sales and share information with them for the first time.

■ Have all orders entered into the new CRM system, which will have a two-way interface to the ERP system.

■ Grant channel partners shared access to customer and order information.

■ Some of the above.

■ All of the above.

And, of course, the more ambitious the deliverables, the greater the project staffing – anywhere from 10 to 30 or more consultants – and the greater the risk, both technical and organizational. Six months and as many million dollars later, reality sets in, and nothing's delivered, or what's delivered is unworkable. And all those benefits that were promised have suddenly disappeared. At which juncture the exec sponsor would be justified in asking 'Who moved my cheese?'

At the end of the day, CRM is a journey, not a destination. It is therefore important to define a set of realistic milestones that take into account the complexities of the terrain and the uncertainties of the road ahead.

HOW TO DEFINE A PHASED APPROACH

In order to plan the journey, first identify your problem areas where the expected benefits are greatest; then adopt a phased approach based on the following rules:

▌ Avoid simultaneous cross-functional deliverables as far as possible, especially when sales is one of those functions (see next point). The nature of CRM is such that all functions (sales, marketing, order management and customer service) have to get used to a radically changed environment, in the form of changed processes, new processes, system changes and training. To try to manage such issues in two functions, each undergoing wrenching change, while at the same time ensuring things work back and forth between those functions, is really pushing the risk envelope, to put it mildly.

▌ A logical conclusion from the first point: do not plan for any cross-functional system interfaces for day one. If you plan to automate your sales cycle, which currently throws paper order forms over the wall to order management, then continue that over-the-wall relationship until your sales cycle is stable. If you need to associate new leads with valid campaigns from the marketing system, then include a field in the sales system with a static drop-list of the current campaigns (of which there are never more than a handful anyway). Ditto if you need the most recent pricing to enter a valid order, and your pricing structure is simple and doesn't change every few weeks. If on the other hand you have a complex and/or highly volatile pricing structure, then you might not be able to avoid an interface. But the first line of reasoning should always be to schedule interfaces for a later phase, especially if the system you're replacing doesn't have an interface anyway. Lastly, note that in some sectors you cannot avoid interfaces, eg banking and insurance, where transactional customer information is held in back-office systems.

▌ Start as far as possible with the sales function because: 1) it is by far the most difficult CRM component because of the difficulty of obtaining buy-in from the sales force; 2) it is an essential two-way link, to marketing upstream and to order management downstream. Until your sales force has a stable sales cycle adequately supported by a sales tool, CRM is not going to happen.

▌ Once the sales function is stable, integrate marketing into a shared data environment, ie a common customer/prospect database, with clear roles and responsibilities for data ownership and data quality. Note that if the sales function is heavily dependent on leads from marketing, as in an SME or SOHO environment, then there might be no alternative but to include both marketing and sales in the scope for day one deliverables. Needless to say, the risk needs to be managed.

❚ Once sales and marketing are integrated, you can move on to order management and customer service.

❚ Keep channel partners for last. Get your own house in order and functioning smoothly before trying to handle third-party sales forces.

Lastly, an important qualifier: the dangers of cross-functional deliverables for day one do not mean that the CRM project is not cross-functional! A CRM project team is by definition cross-functional, since all parties have to agree to the strategy and the long-term objectives. However, actual deliverables are something else altogether. A cross-functional project team can decide on deliverables phased by function, which doesn't change the cross-functional nature of the project.

CHAPTER SUMMARY

❚ Keep the project scope to a reasonable set of objectives that will enable you to show quick results and get the credibility and support essential for the long road forward.

❚ Avoid as far as possible simultaneous cross-functional deliverables, which run the risks of process breakdown across functions, potentially serious bottom-line impact and the project eventually stalling or failing altogether.

❚ Avoid as far as possible automatic interfaces between systems and functions for day one (but do acknowledge the requirement and ensure it is visible in the subsequent phases of the project plan).

7

A realistic budget

I get so tired of listening to one million dollars here, one million
dollars there. It's so petty.

(Imelda Marcos, quoted in MacHale, 1997)

If you do all the right things on the other CRM fronts, it would be a
pity to be caught short because of insufficient funding! Most CRM
budgets are underfunded, often hopelessly so. And the main
reason is ignorance about the real costs of these types of project.

WHY MOST CRM PROJECTS ARE UNDERFUNDED

Since most CRM initiatives are IT-led, IT-partnered or IT-inspired,
the task of defining the budget usually falls to IT. This is reasonable,
since the most visible expenditure will be for the traditional things
like software licences, hardware and consulting. However, being
new to CRM projects, IT understandably fall prey to hidden costs,
and make a number of big mistakes:

▋ They seriously underestimate the number of data sources that need to be migrated over, and the corresponding quality. This results in the migration phase becoming virtually a project in its own right, adding three months or more to the project schedule and requiring additional resources for consulting, cleaning, deduplicating and purchasing new data.

▋ They seriously underestimate how consulting costs can spiral out of control when there is no cross-functional agreement on business processes. This results in a lot of additional work, as consultants and the business scramble to start defining things that the integrator's methodology assumed were already known.

▋ They are unaware of, or underestimate, certain business-related line items that are not present in other types of projects, which consequently fall through the cracks. These include: 1) user training on a far greater scale than what they're used to; 2) resources for change management, to drive process change and ensure data quality; 3) resources for data operations, to manage the importing and exporting of data.

▋ They see the budget as a means to drive a project through to implementation only, after which time the project is assumed to be either self-sufficient or able to wait until the next budget cycle for subsequent funding.

This results in one or more of the following:

▋ The project runs out of money before implementation, and is dependent on a bailout for completion.

▋ The project is scaled back in terms of deliverables in order to meet implementation deadlines.

▋ The project is implemented, but has no ongoing funding, and is therefore dependent on a bailout until the next budget cycle.

This chapter will expose the hidden line items that will enable you to define a CRM budget that doesn't leave you exposed six months down the line.

ANNUAL OR LIFE CYCLE BUDGET?

In an ideal world, you should be able to define and get budget approval for a CRM project over its complete life cycle (or at least two or three years of it). However, not all companies work that way, especially for 'IT projects', which is how CRM is generally viewed today.

Some CRM budgets will therefore be defined annually – with the attendant risk that next time round you won't get the funding you request, in which case you'll have to scale back the project. It is therefore essential that the first year's budget be realistic, otherwise your budget request for the following year will not be viewed as credible.

CAPEX VS OPEX

Different countries have different accounting rules concerning what can be capitalized (capex – capital expenditure) and what must be expensed (opex – operating expenditure, also called SG&A, for salaries, general and administration). For example, US accounting rules state that the costs of people working on systems design, software development and testing can be capitalized, whereas requirements analysis, training and support have to be expensed. This is valid whether the people are company employees, contractors or consultants. In some European countries however, there are variations, eg the above rules would only apply to contractors and consultants, not company employees, whose salaries would be expensed regardless of what phase of the project they're working on.

If you are 'financially challenged' concerning the terms 'capital' and 'expense', here is a quick four-point primer:

▌ A capital cost represents an 'asset', which is something tangible that can be used over a number of years of 'useful life', over which time it has a price or value. It therefore figures on a company's balance sheet, and can be sold or transferred if required, eg computer hardware or an entire factory. The capital cost of an asset is therefore spread out, or 'depreciated', over its useful life.

▌ An operating expense, however, is a one-off cost, which doesn't translate into anything tangible, ie it has no intrinsic 'value' after the fact and cannot be sold or figure on a balance sheet, eg a training session or a business lunch.

▌ From a purely financial perspective for the current financial year, capital costs 'cost less', because they are spread out over a number of years. Operating expenses, however, are 'real costs', which hit the bottom line in full. For example, if the software deliverable of a CRM project is going to cost US $5 million in the first year and can be used over a useful life of five years, its capital cost will be 'only' US $1 million for the first year's budget. If not capitalizable, however, it will hit the first year budget for the full cost of US $5 million.

▍ In conclusion, the more capital-intensive you can 'make' your budget, the less it will 'cost' you this year, and the easier it should consequently be to get approval.

At the end of the day, it's therefore a numbers game. For example, at one of the multinationals I worked for, the capex/opex game reached ridiculous proportions: getting any form of capital for IT projects was relatively easy (eg software development staff), but funding for training and support was parsimoniously distributed. This led to the ludicrous situation in which IT would deliver projects for which it was then unable to carry out proper training and support! As if this were not enough, the IT budget was 100 per cent capital, and all operating expenditure was granted on the fly during the year, usually 'on credit'. So regularly during the year, we'd have opex fire drills where we'd be asked to reduce the funding for training and support for the fully capitalized projects we were to deliver a few months later!

When defining a CRM budget, therefore, one of the biggest mistakes one can make is to emphasize the capex component (which normally gets approved relatively quickly) to the detriment of the opex component (which will be closely scrutinized, and subject to lengthy approval times). The bad news is that the serious underfunding of CRM projects is all on the opex side.

It is important not to proceed with a CRM project until both capex and opex budgets are approved. Otherwise you're playing a high-risk game that could threaten the outcome of the project.

WHAT TO BUDGET FOR

This section will make just a passing reference to traditional project costs, and focus on the hidden costs for CRM projects.

Traditional costs:

▍ software licences and maintenance;

▍ hardware;

▌ consulting;

▌ systems integration (ie package configuration, customization, implementation and integration to other systems);

▌ application training by the package vendor (for IT and other members of the project team).

Hidden costs:

▌ data migration;

▌ user training on a much larger scale;

▌ change management;

▌ data operations.

Data migration

If there's one truism about data, it would be 'No matter how bad you think your data is, it's worse'. The migration of your existing customer and prospect data from their current systems to the new CRM system is one of the key phases of the project.

You will probably have multiple data sources (Access, Filemaker Pro, Excel, previous SFA systems etc) scattered across multiple locations, with different formats and varying levels of cleanliness. In many cases, these multiple data sources are unknown at the time the budget is defined, and only come out of the woodwork once the project is under way.

This results in a data migration phase that, at the extreme, can become a project in its own right, adding three months or more to the project schedule and requiring additional resources for consulting, cleaning, deduplicating and purchasing new data.

This budget line should therefore be based on a complete inventory of all data sources and their corresponding levels of quality. And since the level of quality at this stage can only be a reasonable estimate, you will still need to build in a contingency factor. As a general conclusion, unless you're starting from scratch with freshly purchased data, it can be safely assumed that the migration phase can be expected to last at least two to three months in elapsed time, and will require at least two full-time resources. In most cases this will be true even with a single source of data. For multiple data sources, and especially multiple locations (eg regional offices), this phase can run for as long as six months.

User training on a much larger scale

Whatever training you've had to plan for on other projects, even ERP, it probably still won't prepare you for CRM training, especially for the sales force (which covers the vast majority of CRM projects). For non-CRM projects, logistics for user training is relatively simple, like finding an empty meeting room a few weeks beforehand, installing some PCs connected to the LAN and then locking the door behind you. During that time the trainer prepares the course, period.

   If only it were that simple for CRM:

▌ The logistics of scheduling sales teams from various parts of the country to attend training sessions they'd rather not be at, with confirmation of attendance provided at the last minute, is virtually a full-time job.

▌ This sometimes needs to be done in conjunction with consultants or trainers from training companies, who usually need three to four weeks' notice (with stiff penalties for last-minute cancellations, which will happen and which you can always try to pass on to the sales director).

▌ Reservations of training rooms, either in-house or at off-site facilities, also require at least a month's notice (with similar penalties for cancellations).

▌ IT needs to install PCs, plus one or more of the following: printers, hand-held devices, a LAN connection and dial-up connections – which can sometimes only be done the day before. And then they need to be on-site during the day to provide support.

▌ This needs to be coordinated with the data team who have to prepare the reps' territory data. This is usually loaded the night before, or during the day the training takes place, so that the team can start working right after training.

▌ If the sales force have never used laptops before (not that unusual, even today), or receive a new configuration, a non-negligible amount of time will be spent teaching them how to replace a battery, how to attach/detach the unit from the docking station, how to use 'Caps Lock', dialling in via a modem, etc – in short, training that has absolutely nothing to do with CRM but is nonetheless a prerequisite.

▌ Then there's international training, which should normally be done in each country in the local language (discussed later in this chapter), which means a train-the-trainer approach, with multiple trainers in multiple countries and the corresponding costs for training materials (copying, printing and binding).

▌ And all of this doesn't yet take into account offline usage using a synchronization module, which requires a whole new set of logistics to retrieve reps' laptops the morning they arrive for training, load their software and data during the training session, and give them back to them after the training, at which time they'll realize that some of their non-standard software is no longer working.

All of this, as you can imagine, costs bucketsful of money when compared to training on non-CRM projects. When defining this budget line, therefore, ensure you get input from people who've done it before.

Change management

What is change management?

Change management is usually the most forgotten line item in a CRM budget. It refers to those resources within the business (and not in IT) responsible for:

▌ Defining training from a business perspective, rather than from a mechanistic, button/screen perspective, eg a day in the life of a sales rep. The rep needs answers to questions like: 'How do I retrieve leads from marketing?', 'How do I handle channel conflict with dealers?', 'How can I get the most recent pricing information before I call up a prospect?', etc. These are business questions that require business answers.

▌ Proactively driving process change. Process change is about getting the users to use the CRM tool based on new or changed business processes. When issues arise, either the processes, or the tool, or both, need to be adjusted. This can only be managed by the business.

▌ Ensuring data quality (customers, prospects, orders). With manual methods or islands of automation, users were all in charge of their own data – data quality, like hygiene, was a personal affair. A CRM tool, however, requires that all people share the same data. This results in questions like: 'Who owns the data – sales or marketing?', 'Who has access to what?', 'Who can change this or that?', 'Who has the last word on key customer data like name, address, parent affiliation, etc?', 'Who reassigns accounts or changes territory assignments?', 'Based on whose say-so?', 'How come I don't see account ABC in my list any more?', etc. The business has to set up a data organization to answer such questions and to provide the users with reliable data – the essential ingredient without which their CRM tools won't work.

▊ Providing level one support, which is invariably business support answering the above questions. Level two support is usually technical support provided by IT.

▊ Being the point of contact for IT and for the users. When IT and the business talk to each other, they must do so in a focused and coherent manner, using an official point of contact within the business.

Why change management is often underfunded

In the absence of any explanation on the subject, change management is mistakenly thought of as 'IT support'. In most projects, change management is only brought to people's attention after the budget has been defined. If the additional funding cannot be provided, then the project limps along until the next budget cycle, or simply grinds to a halt.

For international projects, this is further exacerbated by the expectation that everything should be centrally funded. While this is usually the case for software licences, consulting, implementation and IT costs, it is rarely so for in-country change management resources. Whether the organization is based on international operating companies (with a managing director responsible for sales in each country) or lines of business (which cut across geography), there are always budget and headcount restrictions in the countries. With no funding for the project, countries are therefore unable or unwilling to provide the resources for this critical function (see Chapter 13, Case study 3). In the absence of adequate change management resources, the business usually only starts putting people in place when the problems with buy-in and data quality become too big to ignore.

How to estimate change management resources

Here's a rule of thumb for change management resources for sales and marketing (customer service is less impacted because in an integrated CRM environment it would work with clean data provided by sales and marketing).

For a sales and marketing function of 50 people (45 sales and five marketing), you should budget for a total of three to five full-time resources. Because of the high level of business knowledge needed, these should be company employees. Consultants or contractors may be used to facilitate and capture information under the management of company employees, but fully outsourcing this function is a waste of money: when all that carefully acquired business knowledge walks out the door six months later, you have to start all over again.

The breakdown for these resources would be as follows: 1) process change, training and level one support – two or three people; 2) data procedures and data quality – between two and five people. In general you'll need more people for business units in the low-end segments like SME, SOHO and consumer markets, and less for high-end segments like corporate, wholesale and global accounts. This is because of the higher data volatility, volume of external data purchases, and frequency of marketing campaigns at the lower end of the market.

Once the total sales and marketing numbers go over 100 users, the change management numbers will peak off at between five and ten people. Organizationally, these people will be part of either sales support or business operations. However, who they report to is less important than ensuring they exist somewhere in the organization.

Change management for international projects

For international projects, the above numbers would apply for each country. It is tempting to think that processes, training and support can be centralized internationally, eg for process change, have one international group with the equivalent of roving envoys in charge of process change across all countries. This is a pipe dream. The world is a patchwork of different cultures, currencies, languages and legal systems, and the only process change that will be accepted in a country is change that is orchestrated by people who know the local language and the local business culture. Ditto for training and support (which will be taken up in detail in Chapter 8 on international projects).

Data procedures and data quality can be centralized or decentralized as a function of market segment. A central team managing data purchases for all countries is feasible for the high-end segments (corporate, global), but not for the low-end ones (SME, SOHO, consumer), for the following reasons: 1) The small number of fairly stable accounts for the high-end segments (tens of thousands) by definition comprise large national or international accounts, often with cross-border affiliations. Such data can be purchased internationally from a single data provider, and can therefore be managed centrally. 2) For the low-end segments, however, there are numerous accounts (millions per country) that are by definition local. They are therefore purchased from specialized local list brokers. It should come as no surprise to learn that there is no single international data provider capable of providing, for example, the 50 million to 100 million SME companies with five to 30 employees across 15 European countries. Though in theory you could have a central site managing such data suppliers for the European market, in practice it would be difficult to find the right people, and one would be hard pressed to quantify the business benefits of such centralization. Low-end segment data is therefore necessarily decentralized, and managed locally.

Lastly, international projects also require resources for process coordination between countries, and ensuring that there is a balance between top-down strategic requirements and bottom-up country requirements. These are also dedicated posts, and cannot be added on to an existing job description. In the international project of Case study 3 (Chapter 13), for example, these roles were initially assigned to existing people, who needless to say were unable to carry them out correctly. One year later, they all became dedicated posts: one for each country and, at HQ, one for each market segment.

Data operations

What is data operations?

Data operations is about bulk data that cannot be managed manually. It consists of loading and updating information like accounts, contacts, opportunities, activities and campaigns, in such a way as to ensure data coherency and data cleanliness. This is done via templates (manual, semi-automatic or automatic), which are controlled ports of entry from a variety of sources and media into the CRM tool.

This can be broken down into the following types of data tasks:

▌ Importing a set of data that has been cleaned, deduplicated and validated by the business. Such data are usually purchased from an address broker or extracted from another system.

▌ Account reallocation. Accounts usually belong to a team of people, with a primary owner who is usually the sales rep or account manager. When a whole territory has to be reallocated or an account manager leaves the company, the resulting reallocation can be quite complex. Primary account information might need to be reallocated, but not necessarily other related information like opportunities, activities and contacts.

▌ Mass updates of certain fields, eg a national area code update for telephone numbers, or changing account names into upper case.

▌ Recurring tasks, eg daily transfers of campaign information and responses to and from external call centres.

▌ Recurring reports based on consolidated data, eg a monthly win/loss analysis of opportunities, or a weekly funnel report.

▌ Non-standard or one-off tasks, like deleting a list of accounts and related information, or merging accounts and related information.

Data operations staff work closely with the data quality and data procedures staff (identified in the previous section on change management).

Why data operations is often underfunded

Data operations is a specialized area of sales and marketing systems, whose existence most people are not aware of unless they've already automated these functions: hence their general absence as a line item in CRM budgets.

In addition, data operations functions are not visible to the end user and to the people evaluating CRM tools; few evaluations even cover them. Very few CRM tools therefore address these requirements and, when they do, they're not very good. Clients therefore usually end up having to build their own tools and templates to manage data operations. This role usually falls to IT (and sometimes to the change management team in the business), which has to staff up quite significantly.

How to estimate data operations resources

As for data quality and data procedures discussed previously, the rule of thumb for the size of this group is that it is directly proportional to the market segment: in general, the low-end market segments (SME, SOHO, consumer) with their higher data volumes, volatility and marketing campaigns require more people. For the high-end segments (ie corporate, wholesale and global accounts), with their much lower number of named accounts, which are fairly stable, the size of this team could be less than half when compared to the lower-end segments.

Actual numbers can therefore vary from around five to 15 people. For the international telco in Case study 3 (Chapter 13), for example, the IT centre of excellence responsible for sales and marketing systems for three business units across 17 countries had a data operations group of 12 to 15 people. These high numbers resulted from the creation of a third business unit to address the SME market segment; prior to this, when the company was only targeting the high-end segments, this team was around eight people.

For companies whose customer base includes both high- and low-end segments, it is recommended that a single team manages both. Not only would this enable better efficiency and knowledge transfer, it would also prevent the occurrence of data quality issues that arise from organizational turf wars in which each side is overly protective of its market segment to the detriment of the end user.

Data operations for international projects

Because the creation of data templates, import procedures etc is directly related to the data model of the CRM solution, it follows that data operations is a centrally managed IT function.

WHO SHOULD OWN THE BUDGET, IT OR THE BUSINESS?

As CRM is a business-benefits project supported by IT, you could say that either one could own the budget: IT would pay for the traditional items like hardware, software and consulting, and the business would pay for the new line items like training, change management and the purchase of new data.

However, in the real world, money is power, and whoever holds the purse strings calls the tune. And since IT is in the service of the business, and not the other way round, it would make better sense for the business to own the budget in its entirety. Unfortunately, this is rarely the case, so in all probability you will be part of an organization in which IT owns all or most of the budget.

In the case of the budget being shared by the business and IT, you should avoid presenting two separate budgets, ie one for IT and one for the business, each with its own approval process. However, if that's the way your company operates, then the interdependency between the two should be made clear.

HAVE SEPARATE BUDGETS FOR THE PILOT AND THE ROLL-OUT

In the next chapter we will be talking about the vital importance of preceding any CRM roll-out by an operational pilot. When budgeting for a pilot, the usual practice is to include the budget as part of the overall project budget. This should be avoided; it actually makes more sense to separate the two budgets, for the following reasons:

▌ Since a pilot can take place on an inexpensive LAN-based server, which is not necessarily part of the target architecture, and involves around 15 to 30 users only, it can cost around 10 times less than the full project. In an age of expensive IT projects and the statistical risk of failure, a pilot approach is also financially more prudent, and will be much appreciated by the CFO. Obtaining such funding should therefore be relatively quick and easy.

▌ Even by applying all the rules in this book and elsewhere, the sheer magnitude of CRM projects means that it will always be difficult to come up with an accurate project budget. You can only start getting a feel for the real numbers about three to six months into the project. A final project budget calculated after a successful pilot will therefore be much more accurate – and especially more credible.

▌ From a risk standpoint, with only one in five CRM projects succeeding these days, an unsuccessful US $500,000 pilot would not be the end of the world – unlike an unsuccessful US $5 million embarrassment with potential bottom-line impact.

▌ A working pilot, with clearly measurable benefits and fully supported by the business, is a virtual guarantee for approval of the rest of the project. The 30 to 50 pages of complex and tortuous ROI justifications that would shuttle back and forth for many months between the sponsor and finance before a green light is eventually obtained (maybe) would be replaced by a five-page summary that essentially says 'Refer to ROI figures published for the pilot (and by the way make it quick because we need to keep up the momentum of this successful project)'.

Depending on how far into the annual budget cycle the pilot takes place, you will want to take the precaution of obtaining an interim budget between the end of the pilot and the start of the full project, to ensure that the project doesn't lapse between the two.

NO MEGA-LICENCE DEALS BEFORE A SUCCESSFUL PILOT

As a logical conclusion from the previous section, you'll want to avoid any enterprise-wide deals for software licences before a successful pilot. Many years ago, before the reality of CRM project success rates became public knowledge, most companies would sign mega-deals with CRM vendors for thousands of multi-site licences, often on an international scale. Swept up in the euphoria of the times, they went for the biggest discount by purchasing across the board, firmly convinced that within a year at the most virtually the whole company would be using the software. What happened instead was that, as the projects began to fail, companies ended up carrying very expensive inventory in the form of unused licences (subject to 20 per cent annual maintenance fees).

This significant upfront financial commitment also had the unfortunate result of forcing the company into a headlong rush forward – never mind into what, as long as everyone was seen to be working on the project. It was politically impossible to take the time to pause, step back, see the results of the first phase and perhaps adjust the timing or nature of the second phase.

Companies today seem to be adopting a much more cautious approach. In early 2000, for example, after a successful international implementation of a major CRM product, we (the company I was working for) granted a reference visit to a prospect. Accompanied by the vendor and two consultants, they explained to us that only after carrying out a successful pilot would they commit to signing a licence deal with the vendor. Needless to say, both the vendor and the consultants were extremely focused on the desired outcome.

So never mind about trying to get the best discounts by signing upfront licence deals; first do a successful pilot. You can always work in a clause for a subsequent discount to take into account the pilot licences, which usually account for less than 10 per cent of the total licence count anyway.

WHAT FINAL NUMBERS TO EXPECT

Total project costs, including both business and IT, start at around US $3,000 per user per year and can go all the way up to US $15,000 or more. While it is difficult to estimate what your numbers will be, as this depends on project scope, current infrastructure, product, and integration approach, what you can be reasonably sure of is what the lower limit should be. If your total costs end up at less than US $5,000 per user per year, then take the time to revisit your calculations and try to end up with at least that number – which even then you might want to adjust further depending on the risk analysis score for your project at the end of this book.

Another rule of thumb is to estimate your total implementation costs (ie from project launch to go-live) as five times the cost of your software licences. It could be less, it could be more, but five represents an acceptable average. So if you're spending US $1 million on licences, you can expect a total implementation budget of around US $5 million, ie a total project cost of US $6 million.

CHAPTER SUMMARY

▌ If you're unable to get initial budget approval over the life cycle of your project, it is essential that the first year's budget be realistic, otherwise your budget request for the following year will not be viewed as credible.

▌ It is important not to proceed with a CRM project until both capex and opex budgets are approved. Otherwise you're playing a high-risk game, which could threaten the outcome of the project.

▌ Beware of the hidden costs of data migration, user training, change management and data operations.

▌ The data migration phase can in the extreme become a project in its own right, adding three months or more to the project schedule and requiring additional resources for consulting, cleaning, deduplicating and purchasing new data.

▌ User training for the sales force is logistically very complex and therefore expensive when compared to training on non-CRM projects. When defining this budget line, therefore, ensure you get input from people who've done it before.

▌ Change management resources (to define training from a business perspective, drive process change and ensure data quality) are usually the most forgotten line item in a CRM budget. In the absence of adequate funding, the project either limps along until the next budget cycle or simply grinds to a halt.

▌ Data operations, which automates the import and export of bulk data, is essential to ensure data coherency and data cleanliness. This role usually falls to IT, which should budget appropriately.

▌ Ideally, the business should own the CRM budget in its entirety. If, however, the budget is shared by the business and IT, each with its own approval process, then the interdependency between the two should be made clear.

▌ Have separate budgets for the pilot and the roll-out: it will be approved much more quickly, is less risky and if successful will speed up approval for the rest of the project.

▌ Avoid signing mega-licence deals before a successful pilot. In the event of failure, you risk carrying very expensive inventory in the form of unused licences (subject to 20 per cent annual maintenance). You can always work in a clause later for a discount to take into account the pilot licences purchased initially.

▌ If your total costs are less than US $5,000 per user per year, take time to revisit your budget calculations. Another rule of thumb is that total implementation costs should be around five times the cost of your software licences.

8
Successfully managing international CRM projects

Heaven is a place where the police are English, the cooks French,
the engineers German, the lovers Italian, and everything is
organized by the Swiss. Hell is where the cooks are English, the
engineers French, the police German, the lovers Swiss, and
everything is organized by the Italians.

(John Elliot, quoted in MacHale, 1997)

WHY INTERNATIONAL PROJECTS ARE INHERENTLY RISKY

Whether you're implementing CRM, ERP or any other system,
international projects are inherently risky and present an entirely
new set of challenges to the project manager. And these go far
beyond the obvious things like different languages and cultures,
and the need for national language versions of the software.

Since most multinationals are characterized by a hotchpotch of
different systems and data-consolidation headaches, standardized
international solutions are understandably very appealing. The
immediate benefits that come to mind are reduced costs, easy data
consolidation, standard processes and international synergy.

And yet, as anyone who has ever worked on international projects will tell you, good luck – you'll need it! Because, unless your company has some experience in this area, your well-intentioned undertakings stand every chance of backfiring.

Throughout this section, I use the words 'country' and 'subsidiary' interchangeably, whether we're dealing with international operating companies (ie with a managing director responsible for sales in each country) or lines of business (which cut across geography). Apart from the different reporting lines, they otherwise share the same local issues.

International mega-projects usually fail for the following reasons:

▌ *No local buy-in.* Local buy-in into a corporate solution is probably the most important factor in determining whether users will accept a solution. If a country's key users and IT staff are not part of an international process to ensure buy-in, there's an even chance that the resulting corporate solution will die a natural death inside of a year, because it's either unworkable or unwanted. Unfortunately, in most cases countries are not even asked to approve the standard solution, which is more or less imposed.

▌ *Hidden costs.* Though economies of scale and the elimination of duplicate effort are supposed to generate significantly reduced costs, the opposite can actually be true. Once you've factored in coordination costs (people and travel) and the high infrastructure costs associated with running a central solution and keeping it in sync across multiple countries, any upfront cost-savings could well have evaporated within three years.

▌ *Asking for miracles.* Practical considerations like time and money make it impossible to evaluate correctly and implement a one-size-fits-all international solution, suitably modified for the requirements of all subsidiaries. The final solution can only be a compromise, which usually ends up working less well than a local product.

▌ *High political stakes.* The international visibility and high-level commitment associated with such projects make backtracking politically impossible. To err might be human at country level, but in an international context it could be damaging to your career. What locally might be considered an 'acceptable' US $500,000 one-time mistake could, internationally, become a US $5 million a year corporate runaway.

▌ *Local realities.* Time and distance mean that local realities will always win out. Beneath the surface, a combination of inadequate product, company politics and cultural differences sets up a destructive process, ensuring the eventual demise of corporate solutions that do not fit locally. This is especially true in countries that are already advanced in a particular functional area, and are asked to accept a 'dumbed down' international solution that has no chance of outperforming what it already has.

When international projects fail for one or more of the above reasons, the overall view as perceived in the subsidiaries is one of insensitive project management, ie HQ comes in with a 'big-stick corporate project' mentality that places insufficient emphasis on country buy-in and local realities.

International standard solutions can also have some unintended consequences. Firstly, they have the tendency to create self-perpetuating international structures with a vested interest in corporate solutions and standards, which may not always be justified. There are very few corporate IT groups with the vision and the maturity necessary to be able to draw the line between solutions that absolutely must be centralized because it is vital to the health of the company and those that can be decentralized at country level because it makes business sense. Most international structures unfortunately standardize virtually across the board. In extreme cases, you have so-called 'global products and technology' departments staffed mainly by techies for whom adherence to alphabet-soup standards – with a half-life of six months – is more important than local business needs and the presence of adequate in-country support. Such groups spend vast amounts of money defining 'strategic' technical standards from a market of me-too products.

Secondly, by assuming that there is the 'one best way' to do something, it puts a whole company into a product straitjacket, thereby hindering reactivity to changing conditions. In today's market place, there are many 'right' ways of solving a problem, and new products come out regularly. While companies certainly don't always want to be early adopters of new technology, those with heavy investment in international standard solutions inevitably have an enormous amount of inertia to contend with. In the worst-case scenario, they know they should move to something new, but cannot because they are contractually and politically locked into yesterday's solution.

International projects are a risky business with very high failure rates – which understandably are hardly ever publicized. Having personally worked for over 12 years at four multinationals from three different parts of the world (United States, Europe, Japan), at both HQ level and in the countries, I can clearly attest to all of the above. The objective of this chapter, however, is not to come out for or against international projects in general, but to show – rightly or wrongly – to what extent the deck is stacked against them. With this firmly in mind, let us now talk about international CRM projects.

DO INTERNATIONAL CRM PROJECTS MAKE SENSE?

This is such a sensitive question that the only reasonable answer – which also happens to be the most politically correct – is 'It depends'. Just because a company is a multinational, or operates internationally, doesn't mean that an international CRM project makes sense. It depends on the answers to some basic questions about the organization, its customers and its products.

Is there a cross-border customer base?

The most fundamental question concerns the organization and its customer base. Does it operate in a cross-border fashion, ie independently of geography, or not? Let's take the example of the Acme company, which sells widgets internationally, and has sales offices in country A and country B.

If each sales office can sell widgets to customers in both country A and country B, then clearly Acme operates cross-border, since it treats all customers as if they were in one virtual geographical area. It therefore has an international customer base.

If, however, each sales office can only sell widgets to customers in its own country, then Acme does not operate cross-border, since customers are limited to a given geographical area. It therefore has a national customer base in each country.

We can draw three fundamental conclusions here:

▎ Just because a company operates internationally doesn't necessarily mean it operates cross-border, ie it doesn't necessarily have an international customer base.

▌ If a company has a cross-border or international customer base, then the customer-facing functions of sales, marketing and customer service are necessarily based on common processes, common data and common systems.

▌ If a company has a cross-border or international customer base, then the customer-facing organizations of sales, marketing and customer service are either global (ie based in one country and serving the whole world) or regional (ie based in one country and serving a region, eg Europe or Asia Pacific).

Is the service being sold cross-border?

The other key question is whether a service is cross-border, in the sense that it exists across geography, ie the service starts in one country and ends in another. Some examples:

▌ international package delivery services;

▌ international car rental, with drop-offs allowed in another country;

▌ a high-bandwidth, point-to-point telecommunications link between two cities in different countries, linking the branches of an international bank.

Note that products by definition are not cross-border. They are tangible objects that might be manufactured in different countries but are always delivered to a single address. This distinction is important: cars, pharmaceuticals, computers etc might be 'international' products in the broad sense of the term, but they are not cross-border.

When international CRM projects are justified

Now coming back to our original question, 'Do international CRM projects make sense?', if the customer base or the service is cross-border then the answer is definitely 'yes', ie international CRM makes sense – in fact there is no alternative since all countries need to share data at *transactional* level (as opposed to reporting level – the distinction is important, as we'll see further on). Examples are international e-commerce sites, international car rental, international package delivery services etc.

For international e-commerce sites especially (eg Amazon or Dell), the requirement for standardization applies to processes as well as data. Opening systems up to the Internet means that people from many different countries can see and use them. Different processes in this context can be a nightmare, for customers, customer-facing staff and users of reports. As we move to newer technologies in which the size of the screen is reduced significantly (and the visual cues to help users navigate the system are reduced), international standardization will become much more desirable. Businesses like Amazon and eBay, for example, would probably not have achieved the success they have if their interfaces and processes differed between countries.

If, however, the customer base is not cross-border (which usually means the product or service isn't cross-border either), then the answer is 'maybe', ie an international CRM project *might* make sense. This would be dependent on many factors, eg an international strategy for customer communication, marketing, service delivery, customer service, international reporting etc. This could be the case for large, global customers that wish to present a common face across certain functions when dealing with their many international offices. But at the end of the day, international CRM is not a prerequisite, since different countries don't need to share data at a transactional level, and the processes for dealing with customers in each country are usually different.

Are there any other reasons for international CRM projects?

So if neither the customer base nor the service is cross-border, then would there be any other reason for international CRM? Three answers are usually given:

▌ standard processes;

▌ international reporting;

▌ reduced costs.

Let's take a look at these in turn.

Standard processes

Standard processes for CRM would mean that all countries work in generally the same fashion, from marketing through sales through order management, delivery and customer service. This is supposed to increase sales and/or reduce costs, since these standard processes would correspond to so-called 'best practice' for a given industry. However, this theory is based on a number of assumptions, usually unstated:

▮ Someone would have to decide, based on experience or otherwise, what constitutes best practice and then prove why it is better than someone else's best practice.

▮ The benefits of switching to best practice must be not just incremental, but better by orders of magnitude, in order to justify the cost and disruption that would accompany such a move.

▮ Best practice can be decided centrally, and imposed internationally.

▮ Because standardized central processes by definition have more inertia than local processes, they will always be less reactive to changing market conditions in the countries. But this downside is acceptable, ie any reduced sales or increased costs in a country resulting from the inability to react quickly to changing local conditions will always be significantly less than the overall benefits described in the second point above.

For each of these assumptions, however, reality is quite different:

▮ Best practice is in the eye of the beholder. It is a practical impossibility for anyone to decide what is the one best way to do something across multiple countries (when you hear the words 'best practice', it usually means someone is trying to get you to do something you'd rather not be doing, or something you've never seen but you have to take their word for).

▮ Even assuming everyone could actually agree on the same way of doing something in all countries, the chances are small that it would be orders of magnitude better than existing processes, so as to justify a business case.

▮ You can't impose best practice; people have to buy into it. Anyone who has worked in any large company can confirm how difficult it is even in one country to standardize processes across regional offices. Just think how much more difficult this would be internationally, across different cultures, currencies, languages and legal systems.

▌ When changing market conditions in a country threaten to have negative bottom-line business impact in terms of reduced sales or increased costs, central process benefits suddenly become a non-issue. Any standard solution that does not address the associated business problems in an acceptable time-frame will always be sidelined in favour of a local quick fix.

On the subject of buy-in to international processes, here's a real-world example of an international telco with a European CRM project run out of the UK, in which the French office had dozens of special customizations they claimed were essential for business. In reality, the differences between their processes and the new standard turned out to be more apparent than real. But they were adamant in their demands for modifications. With hindsight, the view of the project manager a year later was that, in the drive for standardization, it is really important to ensure that the users feel that the system will support their 'idiosyncratic' ways of working. Otherwise you lose their buy-in and they either flatly refuse to cooperate or (worse) wait for the next opportunity to drop you in it.

On the subject of best practice, it is worth asking where the best practice comes from. If it is a procedure dictated by a major supplier or major customer who has standardized internationally, then the benefits are usually clear. If, however, it came from a conference of bright young managers, or a committee of experts, or a firm of consultants, it is time to start the sirens and ask for the fully costed business case.

Finally, another downside of standard processes is the assumption of the 'one best way' of doing something, which can put a whole company in a process and software straitjacket, thereby hindering reactivity to changing market conditions. So *'Vive la différence'* is not necessarily heresy.

In conclusion, standard international processes, especially in the front-office environment of CRM, is one of *the* most oversold concepts in modern business, which experience has shown to be unrealistic and generally unachievable. Unfortunately, it still remains one of the most often-used business justifications for international CRM. And because it is so politically correct and supposedly goes without saying, few people dare to question its validity.

International reporting

International reporting is based on consolidated data, as opposed to real-time or transactional data, eg weekly or monthly reporting for key performance indicators, sales forecasting, bookings, billings, backlogs etc. International reporting has absolutely nothing to do with CRM, which is about processes and customers. International reporting is simply about common data – which may or may not come out of common systems. In fact, more often than not, international reporting is based on common data coming out of disparate systems around the globe.

Having said that, the use of a standard CRM solution across countries can enormously simplify international reporting. For example, with everyone working from the same product codes and sales funnel stages, forecasting suddenly becomes trivial. However, such simplified international reporting is simply the by-product of everyone working off common data – regardless of the processes behind the data or whether this has any impact on the customer. For the sales forecasting example above, the actual sales processes in each country are usually different. But as long as they agree to some common data definitions, then simplified international reporting becomes possible.

Can this actually be a driver for CRM? Absolutely – lots of SFA and CRM projects usually have this as one of the drivers. However, it should not be the *main* one (at least not officially). The reason is that the disruption and process change that accompany a CRM project are so great that the best way to sell it is to focus on the productivity and process benefits for the users rather than on reporting benefits for HQ. Presenting international reporting as the main driver for a CRM project is the best way to ensure it is rejected by the very people who have to provide the required information.

In summary, therefore, international reporting should be viewed as a very desirable by-product of a CRM project, or a secondary driver, but certainly not the main driver.

Reduced costs

Reduced costs are also a common argument in favour of international CRM projects. Through economies of scale and the elimination of duplicate effort, as the argument goes, an international project simply has to cost less than multiple initiatives in each country.

This argument is based on a number of assumptions, usually unstated:

▌ Software and hardware form the bulk of the cost equation for CRM projects, and it is mainly this that would generate the economies of scale.

▌ The sum of people costs across multiple countries is prohibitive, and can be reduced through the elimination of duplication of effort, by providing a smaller central team.

▌ The resulting reduction in costs is not just incremental, but orders of magnitude cheaper than the alternative, in order to justify the disruption that would accompany a central system (not to mention the ill will fostered by the decommissioning of existing systems that satisfy local requirements, or the halting of local initiatives for a new system).

▌ Because new versions of a central solution for multiple countries will necessarily take much longer to implement than a local solution (by a factor of three to six months at least), the central solution will always be less reactive to changing market conditions in the countries. But this downside is acceptable, ie any reduced sales or increased costs in a country resulting from the inability to react quickly to changing conditions will always be significantly less than the cost reductions described above.

For each of these assumptions, however, reality is quite different:

▌ Not only do software and hardware represent less than 50 per cent of the cost equation for CRM projects, but a closer examination would reveal that economies of scale are not always possible. A software vendor, for example, would usually provide a very generous discount even for a single country, because of the reference value of the global account name and the potential for future business. The difference between the global discount for a standard worldwide package, and the sum of the discounts obtained in each country for independently chosen CRM solutions would in all probability be either negligible, or not sufficiently important to be worth the bother. On the hardware side, it doesn't necessarily follow that a centralized solution will automatically yield significant cost savings. This would be dependent on a number of factors, mainly the required availability or fault tolerance of the technical environment, and the data volumes (customers, prospects, leads). For example, a centralized data centre might cost less for a high-availability and/or high-volume environment (eg B-to-C), but not necessarily for a low-availability and/or low-volume environment (eg B-to-B). The following example, based on actual numbers from a real-world budget exercise, shows how centralized hardware can actually be *more* expensive than a decentralized solution. The sector is a B-to-B environment in 10 European countries, with an average of 100 users and 100,000 customers and prospects per country. The users all work online, ie there are few or no remote sales reps with the requirement for offline usage with synchronization. Customers and prospects are limited to their national markets, ie there is no cross-border or international customer base (see page 98). High availability or fault tolerance is not a requirement, ie the business could still function if the CRM system were down for 24 hours. Each such country could run any of the market-leading CRM solutions on servers (eg NT) priced at between US $30,000 and US $50,000, without fault tolerance and very comfortably dimensioned for growth. A central solution, however, (probably Unix-based) would have to be fault-tolerant because of the business impact for 10 countries, ie even though each country does not require fault tolerance, with all 10 on a single server this now becomes a necessity. It would also have to be generously dimensioned to ensure adequate response times, and maybe boast a hot site back-up as well. Such a configuration could cost in the region of US $2–3 million easily – or four to six times *more* than the total decentralized hardware costs. And this doesn't even take into account the network infrastructure required for a centralized solution (next point).

▌ The network infrastructure costs required for a centralized solution to provide the required bandwidth for adequate response times around the globe can be very high. Though multinationals already by definition boast an important international MAN/WAN network infrastructure, it will probably not have been dimensioned for simultaneous online access for sales, marketing and customer service users around the world. With a decentralized solution at country level, however, the incremental cost increase required to run a local CRM solution on the existing country network infrastructure (LAN/MAN) is negligible in comparison.

▌ Instead of reducing people costs by eliminating duplication of effort, centralized solutions result in negligible economies in people costs, as a closer examination shows:
– Central solutions cannot be decided in isolation at corporate HQ. They need the cooperation of people in the countries, usually the very same people who would go out and purchase a local solution. There are therefore few economies of scale here.
– There is the additional cost of a central project team required for managing and coordinating a company-wide solution, with associated travel costs.
– Then there are consulting costs, which for a central solution for multiple countries will, by definition, be much more complex and expensive than for local solutions for single countries.
– Finally after implementation, there'd be the infrastructure staff required for coordination and keeping a single solution in sync across multiple countries. This also represents an additional cost.

When adding up the numbers on both sides, it would be highly unlikely for a central solution to generate reduced people costs by eliminating duplication of effort. They would either cancel each other out or result in a difference not significant enough to be worth the bother.

▌ In the light of the above two points, the question of the order of magnitude of cost reductions to justify a business case is a non-issue. As shown above, it can even go in the opposite direction, ie a central solution can over time end up costing *more* than decentralized solutions. (A hybrid approach based on regional and decentralized solutions could represent a compromise – see page 117).

▌ If the increased lead time for a new version of a central solution threatens to have negative bottom-line business impact in some countries (ie reduced sales or increased costs), the central cost-reduction benefits would immediately become a non-issue. The greater such impact in a country, the quicker any standard solution will be sidelined in favour of a local quick fix.

At the end of the day, international hardware and software standards are less important than the impact of those standards on country operations and the bottom line. The coordination costs of centralized solutions should never be underestimated; in the short space of a few years or less, they can very easily exceed upfront cost-savings in software and hardware. And as if that were not enough, they can also have serious operational impact in the countries that are supposed to benefit from them.

Reduced costs through economies of scale and the elimination of duplicate effort, like standard international processes, is another one of *the* most oversold arguments in modern IT, which experience has shown to be unrealistic and generally unachievable. Unfortunately, because it is so politically correct and supposedly goes without saying, few people dare to run through the numbers – at least publicly. So it still remains one of the most often-used business justifications for international CRM.

WHY DO COMPANIES LAUNCH INTERNATIONAL CRM PROJECTS?

Of the three alternative reasons covered above (standard processes, international reporting and reduced costs), only international reporting is really a valid one, and even then only as a secondary driver. So in answer to the question of whether international CRM projects make sense, the answer would seem to be 'Not very often'. Why then are there so many international CRM projects? After all, the market leader in CRM tools is firmly entrenched in large multinationals rolling out its product globally.

The answer is very simple. The main reason is that many international CRM projects are IT-driven, and IT by definition focuses on 'standard systems'. The standardization of the software and hardware components of CRM via the cost-reduction argument becomes the implicit driver, which then teams up with that other inescapable driver, standard processes. Even for those international CRM projects that are truly business-driven, the cost-reduction and standard processes arguments invariably dominate, because in the absence of any serious comparative analysis they 'go without saying'.

In summary, any international project is inherently risky. International CRM projects, because they target front-office functions that are usually not as process-oriented as traditional back-office functions, are several orders of magnitude more risky. Unless there is a real and justifiable business case for data sharing based on cross-border activity and/or cross-border services, the firm recommendation should be to skip it. Let each country proceed with its own CRM initiative, suitably coordinated to ensure common data, synergy and a healthy exchange of 'best practice' (in the sense of multiple 'best practices'), but with no obligation except the requirement to provide international reporting based on common data.

CRITICAL SUCCESS FACTORS FOR INTERNATIONAL PROJECTS

If for whatever reasons, justified or not, your company has embarked on an international CRM project and you have to run it, then here are the steps you must take to reduce the risks and ensure that the 'international factor' does not stand in the way of a successful project.

Successfully managing HQ/country relations

The 'great divide' between HQ and countries is a classic, and is the first visible obstacle a project manager comes up against in an international project. For those of you who have not worked in an international environment – at both HQ *and* subsidiary level to get a balanced view – this is what you would be up against.

Using a farming analogy, people in HQ usually view themselves as enlightened people from the city, with an obligation to help the struggling farmers out in the countries. They always have initiatives under way that, though well intentioned, are usually out of touch with local realities and rarely deliver tangible results. Back in the countries, people view HQ as city folk who try to teach farmers how to grow potatoes. They politely hear them out (after all, HQ does provide welcome funding) but, at the end of the day, they'd much rather be left alone to get on with their business.

OK, it's a caricature, but like all caricatures it's rooted in reality. After all, people from corporate HQ dropping in on the countries are not exactly well known for asking the locals what they need and trying to address those requirements. The norm is rather to tell people what they need and what's going to happen soon because of this new policy or that emerging strategy. Back in the countries, people are not exactly as pure as the driven snow either. Their vastly superior knowledge of local conditions sometimes blinds them to the fact that they are part of an international business, with international concerns. Still in terms of the farming analogy, people in the countries would probably intensify the growth of potatoes for next year, even when a valid corporate analysis shows that the global market for potatoes is undergoing change and they probably need to start diversifying.

This results in an arms-length relationship, with each side wary of the other, and cooperation a necessary evil. Concealing information, lying by omission and fudging the numbers are therefore all part of the game. Two examples follow: 1) HQ imposes an upper limit for capital project budgets from the countries, above which central approval is required. In the countries, they take this into account by descoping the project to arrive at final numbers just below the limit, or by creating multiple budgets, seemingly unrelated, and staggered over time. 2) If a country is on to a really big potential sales win, it will find a way to under-report the numbers and the actual funnel stage in the sales cycle, in case someone from corporate wants to 'help' close what the country perceives to be a local deal.

Whether we like it or not, therefore, international project teams have to deal with a 'them and us' culture. If you're from HQ, then 'they' are the 'bad guys' and 'we' are the 'good guys'. If you're from the countries, then it's the other way round, with HQ being the big bad wolf. It is vital to point out that whether you agree with this view or not is totally irrelevant at this stage – *your role is to accept it exists and to learn how to deal with it.*

One of the biggest mistakes one can therefore make when running a corporate CRM project from a HQ perspective is to adopt a 'big-stick corporate project' mentality and in effect tell the countries that what they've been doing up to now is wrong, and by golly you're going to show them how to do it right – and by the way, they don't have a choice in the matter! Exaggeration? Hardly – there are more than enough horror stories doing the rounds not to be convinced.

You can start by listing all of your preconceived ideas of how much authority HQ has over countries – and then throw most of them out of the window. You're going to have to learn a new set of rules, which all basically boil down to one thing – *you can't impose a corporate solution; you've got to get buy-in to make it work.* And if you have to bend over backwards to get buy-in, so be it, but that should be your ultimate objective – which at the end of the day is much more important than aggressively meeting centrally defined corporate deadlines without buy-in.

Successfully managing HQ/country relationships can therefore be summed up in two requirements of the project manager. 1) Accept that you are in a difficult role, in which you will be viewed as part of the 'bad guys'. Don't fight it – it's nothing personal against you. That's how multinational politics work, so come to terms with it. 2) Go out of your way to sell both yourself and the project, so as to obtain buy-in. Remember, putting it in place is the easy part; making it work is quite another. It is better to be late with buy-in, than on time with rejection and political ill will.

Get buy-in from all countries

How to get international buy-in can be better understood by looking at a real-world example. My very first international project manager role at a multinational, way back in 1987, saw me with a mandate to install a financial package in the European countries. Being new to such projects, I naturally went in armed with lots of goodwill and a great deal of conviction in the usefulness of what I was been asked to do. Alas, a month into the job and after having visited a few countries, I discovered that, even though the people in the countries were putting in the appropriate effort to meet me to plan the implementations, they were going about it in a half-hearted manner because:

▌ they were not at all part of the decision to choose system ABC, which was a 100 per cent corporate initiative – if it was deemed good for HQ, it would be good for the countries;

▌ the corporate group based their decision on a demo of a future system, which was supposed to come out 'soon' – needless to say, that deadline slipped and in the meantime the company would install the previous version, whose sell-by date had already expired, and would do an upgrade later;

▌ they were not sufficiently staffed to be able to assign people to the project while at the same time doing their normal jobs;

▌ most had no problems with their current systems, and saw no reason to change – though they all agreed that corporate had huge problems closing the books at month end.

Unfortunately all of this didn't change anything – corporate wielded its big stick and, after three implementations fraught with technical difficulties, functional shortcomings, international squabbling and political ill will, the company at last threw in the towel and spared the remaining countries the same ordeal.

As is usually the case when projects end in embarrassing failure, the company accepted it had screwed up royally and did a post-mortem. One year later, when a new project was launched for a corporate financial solution for European countries, it was done so well that a product was selected in under three months with full buy-in from all countries, followed by simultaneous implementations in three countries during the last quarter, enabling the new financial year to start on the new system.

Obtaining country buy-in is not exactly rocket science. It's the same approach you'd use within a single country – only this time you're taking the pains to include everyone else. Here are the main steps:

▌ Identify executive sponsors at business and IT level.

▌ Recruit a project team from the countries.

▌ Define joint requirements.

▌ Evaluate solutions.

▌ Agree on a final solution.

▌ Define the way forward.

▌ Have plenty of face-to-face meetings.

Let's look at these in turn:

▌ *Identify executive sponsors at business and IT level.* You need at least three key people: an executive sponsor, a project owner reporting to the sponsor and an IT project manager. The buy-in phase is jointly run by the owner and the project manager; it is irrelevant who the main player is, as long as they work in concert with each other.

▌ *Recruit a project team from the countries.* The owner and the project manager then recruit the required country representatives: one from the business and one from IT. You usually don't want more than six countries represented; otherwise it becomes too difficult to manage. So the countries usually end up agreeing some sort of representation, either regional (eg Nordic countries, Asia Pac countries) or based on the size of the business in a country (eg 'small' and 'large' countries).

▌ *Define joint requirements.* The project team thus constituted then defines key requirements. This crucial step is a subject in its own right, which is beyond the scope of this book. Suffice to say that you want to keep it as simple as possible, and end up with a document of 30–50 pages maximum, which describes key processes and data. The JAD (Joint Application Design) methodology or equivalent workshop sessions (see page 158) will yield the required deliverables. What you definitely don't want to do is go through a long-drawn-out, bureaucratic, nit-picking process that becomes an end in itself and results in an unreadable 300-page 'statement of requirements'.

▌ *Evaluate solutions.* With documented requirements, you will now be able to evaluate candidate solutions.

▌ *Agree on a final solution.* The final selection should be agreed by all. If the final selection results in IT and the business opting for different solutions, then you've got a clear case of a project team in which IT and the business are not working together, since one or both sides are not taking the big picture into account. A properly conducted evaluation by a cohesive and motivated team inevitably yields a joint winner.

▌ *Define the way forward.* Obtaining buy-in on a standard solution might be the most important step in an international project, but it is only the first in a long journey. An implementation approach (usually based on a pilot – see next section) and a project plan need to be agreed.

▌ *Have plenty of face-to-face meetings.* Having come this far in terms of solid progress, the last thing you want to do at this stage is to limit face-to-face meetings on the grounds of cost savings. Conference calls, videoconferencing and e-mail are not the best media for obtaining international consensus (see page 125). The costs of travel should be viewed as an investment in obtaining consensus, without which no international project can succeed.

Lastly, a qualifier on buy-in: large multinationals are not a fairy tale environment, in which you can always obtain buy-in. Sometimes, you have to wield the corporate big stick. But only do so as a last resort, after you have exhausted all other avenues of communication and persuasion.

On one international project I managed, there were two countries that behind the scenes did not want any part of a corporate solution. The reasons were less to do with any shortcomings in the proposed solution and more to do with the fact that they had already launched their own locally funded initiatives on the sly (one of them had even purchased licences from another CRM vendor and was busy customizing the product at around the same time). Because the political aspects of these initiatives did not sit well with the executive sponsor, he wielded the corporate big stick and killed off both of them. But this was a last resort, when the selling approach clearly didn't work.

Don't let HQ have free access to country data

High on the wish list of people at HQ is the requirement for a standard international solution to be able to drill down into key information in the countries at the click of a mouse. After all, they have to request the very same numbers from the countries anyway, so there isn't anything big-brotherish about this request, is there?

In theory no, but in practice yes, because of the reality of HQ/country relationships discussed previously, and also because of a natural 'paranoia' that exists throughout the sales organization. From the bottom up, sales reps are paranoid about a sales manager having access to 'their' accounts, and sales managers in turn balk at their sales director being able to review their pipeline at will. So it should come as no surprise that sales directors in turn are loath to 'expose' their operations to their boss – especially when that boss sits at HQ in another country.

There is also the business reality of 'creative' sales forecasting. Virtually all sales organizations whose performance is based on quarterly results 'adjust' monthly reporting based on the percentage of sales targets achieved. HQ of course knows that the countries do this, and the countries know that HQ knows. In the absence of new guidelines and policies on 'open' sales reporting that are accepted by all parties, it would be naive to expect that the countries will willingly roll over and accept a new, top-down information hierarchy.

In Case study 3 (Chapter 13), the question, 'Will HQ be able to look at our data without our knowing?' was asked by virtually all countries during the international road show for the corporate CRM solution. This is only natural; whether this squeamishness of being 'exposed' data-wise to HQ is a form of paranoia, or indicative of shady business practices, or whatever, is irrelevant. The reality of the situation is that it seems to pose a problem, period. Before an international CRM project comes along, this is how the countries operate. Suddenly moving to an open, shared data environment is not something that's going to be easily accepted – at least not initially.

So why take a chance of not getting the countries on board because of this? After all, HQ is still going to get real, consolidated data, only it can be 'pushed' out from the countries (ie the country prepares the data or reports and sends them to HQ), instead of 'pulled' in from HQ (ie HQ extracts the required data and prepares the report). The end result is the same.

In conclusion, you must reassure countries, initially at least, that corporate will not take a sneak peek at their numbers. Even if this is not true and you actually intend to go down that route at a later stage (perish the thought!), you should at least start out by respecting this request. Certainly, it will be easier to look at numbers a year later once the system becomes institutionalized. In one of my CRM projects, we actually started off with this closed, 'push' approach to ensure the countries came on board, and two years later they evolved naturally to an open, 'pull' approach, with HQ able to extract automatically the sales forecast without country 'permission'. The initial driver for 'secrecy' disappeared over time.

Aim initially for a single international version

To ensure we're all on the same wavelength when we use the word 'version', let's first distinguish three seemingly related but in reality independent 'versions' of software: versions from a functional perspective, versions from a language perspective and versions from an implementation perspective:

■ *Functional versions.* A company can have a single version of a CRM product used by all countries, ie from a functional perspective, requirements from around the world are addressed by a single international version of the software, eg V1.0 INT. Alternatively, or in addition to the international version, there can be multiple, country-specific versions, ie from a functional perspective, requirements for certain countries would be addressed by a dedicated version for that country or group of countries, eg V1.0 FRANCE for France and V1.0 APAC for Asia Pacific.

▌ *Language versions.* Regardless of how many functional versions may exist, any given country could run its software either in its national language or in the dominant corporate language, usually English. For example, all countries could run a single international functional version in English, eg V1.0 INT ENGLISH. Alternatively, this single international functional version could be translated into one or more national-language versions, eg V1.0 INT FRENCH for France. Or there could be multiple functional versions for different countries, each of which could be either in English, eg V1.0 FRANCE ENGLISH, or more likely in the national language, eg V1.0 FRANCE FRENCH.

▌ *Implementation versions.* Regardless of how many functional versions may exist, or what languages they run in, the software could be physically implemented either in a single instance for all countries (eg a data centre in Amsterdam) or in multiple instances by region (eg a centre in Amsterdam for Europe, and in Hong Kong for Asia Pacific) or in multiple instances by country (ie each country has its own instance).

The various permutations are summarized in Table 8.1.

How to decide? Well, you can be sure of one thing: just about all countries will express the natural desire to have both a country-specific functional version and to have it in their national language. People from the United States will therefore ask for a US-specific version in English, and the French will want a France-specific functional version with screens in French. So no surprises there.

On the implementation side, the desire for a single instance or multiple instances can be driven by either IT or the business: 1) IT

Table 8.1 *The various permutations between functional, national language and implementation versions of a CRM product*

Functional Version	International (1)				Country-Specific (n)			
Language Version	English (1)		National language (n)		English (1)		National language (1)	
Implementation Version	Single instance (1)	Multiple instances (n)	Single instance (1)	Multiple instances (n)	Single instance (1)	Multiple instances (n)	Single instance (1)	Multiple instances (n)

n = multiple

could favour a single instance for reduced support requirements, or multiple instances for better response times and lower network infrastructure costs; 2) the business could favour a single instance for transactional data sharing, or multiple instances for organizational or political reasons ('under country control').

Since there's no such thing as a free lunch, the best way to address these requests is to lay on the table the associated costs and impact to the business. National language versions are becoming less costly and complex to manage, as modern CRM products begin to combine the various language versions into a single technical release. And for a given network infrastructure, single- or multiple-instance implementation is a non-issue (ie technically implementing an identical solution in single or multiple sites is the same, rather like installing software on one PC or multiple PCs on a LAN; it's all automated).

So any additional costs would mainly be generated by multiple functional versions across countries. This would result in:

▌ greater technical complexity, which impacts reliability;

▌ additional IT resources;

▌ longer lead times for new versions.

The business doesn't care much about the first two costs, which it sees as being an IT issue. However, longer lead times for new versions, in the order of at least three months or more, is something they will certainly want to avoid if they can. They will therefore usually trade functionality and language for shorter lead times for new versions.

My recommendation is to avoid refusing anything outright, and to instead propose a phased approach:

▌ *Functional versions.* Unless there are critical or very important country-specific business requirements that would impact country buy-in, then propose a single international version for phase one, on the understanding that for phase two or phase three the application could evolve to become more country-specific. Whether this can actually be achieved later on will depend on a lot of things, especially the success of the first phase. But at least it presents a reasonable compromise.

▌ *National language versions.* Ditto for language. Unless there are critical or very important reasons that would impact country buy-in (an obvious one being a call centre), then propose a standard common language version – usually English – for phase one, on the understanding that for phase two or phase three the application could evolve to local-language versions.

∎ *Implementation versions.* See the next section below for recommendations on international architecture.

Note that for each of the above options, content will be in the local language. For example, even if the screens are in English, the underlying drop lists will be in the local language, eg Mrs in English, Madame in French, etc.

Keep the initial architecture simple

A company embarking on an international CRM project has the option of the following three architectures:

∎ *Centralized.* At the one extreme, you'd have a single instance of the software on a big machine in a single data centre serving all users worldwide. Needless to say, given the large numbers of users across multiple functions, and the business criticality of the interrelated CRM applications, such a target architecture would be extremely complex and expensive, especially in terms of redundancy and network infrastructure. Depending on a multinational's worldwide network and data centre infrastructures, the lead time for such an undertaking can take up to a year or more.

∎ *Decentralized.* At the other end of the spectrum, you could have multiple instances of the same software version in each country, sitting on various sizes of servers, running off the LAN. With users already running off the LAN for other applications, and the relative ease of adding servers to the local data centre, such an architecture could be up and running within three months. One of the main challenges would be to provide adequate bandwidth to regional offices.

∎ *Intermediate.* Between these two extremes, you could have an intermediate approach with strategically located regional data centres, with replication as a further option. Depending on the upgrade needed to the network infrastructure, and the size of existing data centres, and the replication options, such an architecture could take anything from three months to a year.

Which way to go? Well, there are no hard-and-fast rules. Multinationals have vastly different worldwide network and data centre infrastructures, each with their own set of constraints, both technical and organizational. In addition, the task may be simplified by prior experience with global projects, eg ERP. Then there's also the health of the company or the industry, which will dictate how much capital spending can be thrown into new architectures – especially during a recession.

But there are some common-sense recommendations that nonetheless apply:

▌ Avoid making architecture a potential failure point for a CRM project.

▌ Avoid making architecture a key factor in increasing the lead time for project deliverables.

▌ Avoid making architecture a key factor in user dissatisfaction.

At the end of the day, CRM is not about architectures – response times notwithstanding. It is about very difficult organizational and process change – and a 20 per cent probability of success. The overriding concern should be to create the environment for CRM to take hold and flourish in as many countries as possible, and to start seeing benefits as quickly as possible. Architecture must therefore necessarily take a very distant second place behind the urgent necessity of demonstrating quick returns – even if this is 'inefficiently' done with 'duplicate support requirements' on throw away servers running on the LAN in various countries. The main technical requirement at this stage is to provide adequate response times, and if this is to be achieved by throwing inexpensive hardware at the problem, so be it.

New and ambitious international architectures detract from the business-benefits side of the project. Taken to extremes, they can ultimately break a CRM project for reasons that have absolutely nothing to do with CRM.

In conclusion, keep your initial architecture as simple as possible. There is nothing wrong with starting at the low end as a first phase, and migrating later on once the project has started to prove its worth. This is certainly much better than having the 'correct' architecture a year late and a monument to a stalled or failed project.

Ensure training is in the local language

From a purely cost perspective, the attraction is great to provide standard international training in the dominant language – usually English – for all countries. A constant theme throughout this book is that CRM is all about people and processes, and obtaining the buy-in necessary to accept change. And one of the key instruments for this is training. It would therefore seem only natural to do this in the language in which the people conduct their business with their customers.

Delivering such training in English (classroom tuition and course material) reduces by at least 50 per cent the chances of getting the message across – especially for the sales force, a very difficult user population to convince under any circumstances. It also sends a clear signal to the people concerned that this thing called CRM, which everybody is talking about and to which they are to accord the highest priority, maybe isn't that important after all, since the company can't even invest in local-language training.

In the absence of dedicated training staff in each country, local-language training would require identifying local training partners, training their trainers and gradually outsourcing this function, while all the time maintaining the quality of the training programmes by the central training group.

Needless to say, this is much more expensive than one-size-fits-all training in English, but it still represents a drop in the ocean when compared to what it would cost to have to do the training all over again because of the language factor – not to mention the serious damage to project credibility this would cause.

In a real-world example, the Internet business unit of an international telco had an SFA project under way, based on the same product that the telephone business unit had been using for over two years. The London-based project manager opted for standard training in English for sales forces in Europe. By the time the reality check came, it was too late to incorporate local-language training into the project plan. So they had to turn for help to their sister business unit based in Paris, which had adopted a local-language approach from the outset and thus had the required infrastructure in place.

With the exception of countries where English is well established as a second language (eg the Netherlands) don't even think about standardized English-language training for an international CRM project, under the pretext that it is cost-effective. The only cost you should be comparing international training against is the cost of failure, ie of having to do the training all over again in the local language and having to manage the ensuing project delays and credibility crisis.

Ensure level one support is in the local language

As for training, the attraction is great to provide international support in the dominant language – usually English – for all countries, for cost reasons. And as for training, the reasons against doing this are the same: support should be provided in the language in which the people conduct their business with their customers. Note this is true even if the standard CRM solution has screens in English. It's the working language of the country that drives this decision, not the language of the software. Local-language level one support is part of in-country change management resources (see page 87).

Some companies adopt a centralized level one help desk with automatic call routing to people speaking the same language as the caller. This doesn't work because the problem is not just one of language; it is also one of local business knowledge, ie of the local business culture and of local data like territories, accounts, marketing campaigns etc. By definition this can only be found in the country concerned. What happens in such situations is that the country ends up finding the resources to set up the local level one help desk anyway, without which their users would not be able to function properly. So the central help desk ends up receiving hardly any calls, from which one could conclude that application support is negligible or well provided for. In reality, it has simply shifted to where it should have been in the first place. So the most enthusiastic or knowledgeable users on the ground finish up providing *ad hoc* support – with all the lost productivity and disconnected feedback this entails. The best support ultimately comes from these local 'super users' – but they need to be recognized as part of the support process and be included in requirements gathering, testing and post-implementation review processes.

So, in conclusion, setting up a central help desk for an international CRM project, even with call routing based on language, has every chance of being an expensive, underused infrastructure. Level one support is first and foremost business support, not technical support. So ensure the change management budget captures this requirement, so that naturally recalcitrant users won't have yet another excuse to say they don't want to use the system.

Ensure key project people have international experience

Successfully running an international project requires a basic understanding of how other countries function from a cultural and business perspective, and the ability to relate that back to your own culture and country from a comparative, rather than a judgemental, point of view. Well, that's easier said than done! After all, we all have our caricatures about others, the punctual Germans, the arrogant French, the loud Americans, the rude Dutch etc, and the list is as long as our ignorance and our prejudices. Caricatures are of course dangerous when they become generalizations, but used carefully they can be useful because they are necessarily rooted in reality, ie in the sense of how one culture perceives another.

Observing cultural differences is far from obvious. We only see the most visible things at first, like the above caricatures. However, there's much more, to such an extent that the other culture can be saying one thing and you end up understanding something completely different. That wouldn't be a big deal if you were a tourist asking the natives for directions, but if you're in a business context trying to get information to support a major decision then the stakes are entirely different.

Observing and understanding cultural differences so that you can be effective in an international project doesn't come naturally – either you have to be briefed beforehand, or you read up on it, or you've actually lived in a country long enough for it to have become apparent.

Observing cultural differences is one thing; taking them into account, however, is quite another. Once aware of these differences, you could react in a number of ways:

▌ Ignore their 'wrong' way altogether and impose your 'right' way of thinking.

▌ Try to win the other side over to your 'right' way of thinking.

▌ Be 'tolerant' and make a concession to their 'wrong' way of thinking.

▌ Simply see it as two sides of the same coin, remove all judgement, get each side to understand the other's way of thinking and work towards a mutually acceptable solution.

Once you remove the judgement element, as in the last point, and strip away what you feel to be 'right', 'wrong', 'better' or 'worse' about how the other side functions, then you start getting on to some very interesting ground. Every comment you then make about the other culture says as much about your *own* culture. For example, if you're French and you say that Americans are loud in public, you're also saying that French people speak softly in public. Or if you're Italian and you say that Germans are sticklers for punctuality, you are also saying that Italians are more relaxed with time. Or if you say that some Asia Pacific cultures have difficultly expressing opposition or dissent during meetings, you're also saying that Western cultures accept that it is OK to express opposition or dissent in meetings. And so on and so forth. It takes an extremely open mind to be able to turn around the common reaction 'They function like that' to 'We function like this'. When you can actually do that, you are then able to find ways around the differences, because there is no more judgement to colour your reactions.

Here are some of the most common cultural pitfalls that result in misunderstandings between HQ and countries in international projects – especially for companies where the parent is either US or British:

▌ *'It's an international company, therefore everyone should be comfortable speaking English, and English-speaking people shouldn't have to make allowances for this.'* It might be an international company, but all that really means is that it operates internationally. Within each country, business is conducted and the company is run in the local language. The presence of international managers, who may or may not speak good English, does not change this reality. Native English speakers in international meetings should therefore not assume they are in an equivalent US or British meeting just because the meeting is conducted in English. If you speak to Jean, Juan and Jurgen as if you're speaking to John from next door, then you will not necessarily get your message across, and you won't get the feedback you require from them. The solution is to use simple English, cut down on the slang and colloquialisms, repeat and reformulate key messages, and directly ask questions to each participant to ensure that the right messages are flowing both ways. What also helps enormously, even though it is contrary to one of the unspoken rules of multinational language etiquette, is to encourage non-English speakers from the same country to feel free to talk to each other in their own language if they feel the need for clarification. Usually such 'clarification breaks' don't last more than a minute anyway, but they immediately clear the air – and ensure that issues that might otherwise not be raised are actually discussed. Not understanding the German, French or whatever language that is being spoken at rapid pace for a minute is a very small price to pay for gaining trust and consensus.

▌ *'Meetings are the best forums for gaining consensus. So if we get a green light during a meeting, then we can be sure we have agreement for moving forward.'* The objectives of meetings vary across cultures. In the UK and the United States, for example, meetings are primarily forums for consensus and decision making. In some other cultures, however, eg France and other Latin countries, meetings are primarily forums for an exchange of information, which may or may not lead to a decision. In such countries, the more important the decision, the more likely it will be reached behind closed doors – and then announced in a subsequent meeting. So if the chairperson in an international meeting asks the group, 'Are we all in agreement then?' or, 'Does anyone disagree?', all-round silence does not necessarily mean you have agreement. If only because of the language factor (first point above), some people might be hesitant to speak their mind. If in addition that's not how they normally voice dissent (next point), then there are two reasons to be silent. When trying to reach key decisions, people chairing international meetings should do two things: 1) during meetings, ask certain participants directly whether they agree, as in 'Juan, are you comfortable with this decision for your country?', which should bring about the required response; 2) in an offline environment, eg the coffee machine or a meeting room, have a one-to-one discussion of the issues, which is much more conducive to getting culturally reticent participants to open up.

▌ *'Dissent or criticism will always come out during meetings. If it doesn't then you can assume everything's OK.'* Some cultures, eg US, British and Dutch, separate the people from the problem, ie if you criticize someone's idea, you're not criticizing the person. Other cultures, eg the Latin cultures in Southern Europe, tend to view the person and that person's ideas as forming a whole. It is therefore difficult to criticize one without giving the impression of criticizing the other. Then there are some Asia Pacific cultures that show a deference to authority, which makes it virtually impossible to get any 'negative' feedback in a meeting with senior people present – even when such feedback is explicitly requested! The solution here is once again to place the appropriate emphasis on one-to-one discussions in an offline environment, which is much more conducive to getting dissent on the table.

▐ *'It's difficult working with certain nationalities. For example, the Dutch and, to a lesser extent, the Germans are direct to the point of rudeness.'* Let's imagine a language as a multi-layer communications protocol, rather like the famous seven-layer OSI or Open Systems interconnection protocol for networking. At the bottom you'd have the purely functional language that gets the message across, eg 'I agree' or 'I disagree'. On top of this fundamental layer can be one or more additional layers whose role is to provide nuance, politeness, respect, the ability to accentuate the positive, eliminate the negative, etc. Different cultures have different 'communications protocols' with different numbers of layers. So in answer to the question, 'Do you agree with the proposed plan?' answers can vary: 'No' or 'No, I disagree' or 'I don't disagree, but...' or 'What I like about this plan is...; however, I have reservations about...', etc. But at the purely functional communication level, they're all ultimately saying the same thing. The Dutch and the Germans communicate at lower levels than, say, the French or the British. If you're not aware of this, then what you'd normally interpret as rudeness from someone who speaks to you with the same 'communications protocol' is actually not so at all. Mentally adjusting to this in real time is quite difficult, and only comes with practice. The only solution here is to read up on the basics of the cultures you're likely to be working with, so that you know what their normal way of speaking is (see 'Further reading').

▐ *'We don't need to provide all the details in order to gain agreement to move forward. We can always make adjustments later as a function of progress; the important thing is to focus on the desired result and to get moving.'* This 'just do it' approach, in which you can get started once you are directionally correct, since you can make adjustments as the project moves forward, is mainly a US approach to work. In such a results-oriented culture, risk is acceptable and it is OK to change things on the fly – at worst you fail and start over again. In many European cultures, however, though the term 'risk-averse' would be an exaggeration, failure is less socially acceptable. Therefore, how one plans to move forward, ie the actual processes and not just the desired result, is also important. So in order to start a major initiative, some cultures need to cover much more ground in terms of planning before being able to commit to something big. The English saying, 'We'll cross that bridge when we come to it', does not translate well into some languages. So it is important for people to realize why some cultures seem impatient to get started even when it is patently clear that key information is missing, and why other cultures seem to 'drag their heels' and don't seem to want to reach a decision. Once again the only solution here is to read up on the basics of the countries you're likely to be working with, so that you know how their business culture works.

▌ *'Apart from the fact that there's no face-to-face contact, conference calls by telephone are like meetings, and should be just as productive.'* The problems already covered for meetings above are magnified several times over for conference calls. Expecting international agreement or consensus on key issues on a conference call is unrealistic. Such a forum should mainly be used for exchanging information and providing group updates. Project managers requiring agreement on key issues should take the time to do one-to-one phone calls or e-mails with countries beforehand to build consensus – which can then be confirmed via a conference call.

▌ *'Discussion forums and Web chat are an appropriate medium to get international feedback.'* Experience shows that participation in discussion forums on groupware or the Internet is very ineffective in getting international feedback. I've participated in such forums in several multinationals, and 90 per cent or more of all postings were from native English-speaking countries. Chat and forums are therefore clearly non-representative. The reasons are multiple, but the language factor is clearly dominant. By all means start up such online forums, but monitor the usage and, if you can't get internationally representative feedback, find ways to do so or close the forums down altogether.

The above factors are but the tip of the iceberg; there are many more opportunities for misunderstandings that at best affect the smooth running of a project and at worst can generate a climate of misunderstanding that can threaten the whole outcome. Having worked almost all of my career in an international environment, I have seen first-hand the negative effects of such misunderstandings.

Here are two real-world examples. 1) *Meetings.* A US or British manager is exasperated because, two days after supposedly reaching agreement in a meeting, some continental European colleagues come back with some further issues that prevent them from proceeding. Not surprisingly, a combination of language and cultural barriers to dissent prevented these issues from being put on the table during the meeting. 2) *'Rudeness.'* A manager in London almost fell out with a manager from the Netherlands, whose 'attitude', bordering on 'rudeness', he just couldn't stand. He took it personally and, when he spoke to me about it, I first had a good-natured laugh at his expense, and then explained that it was all cultural, and proceeded to show him examples of conversations and e-mails I'd had with the very same person and some other Dutch managers. He came to the conclusion that he had grasped the wrong end of the stick.

Very few companies (and even that's a liberal estimate) make international experience and exposure an active requirement for international projects. When internationally experienced people do end up in key positions, it is more by accident than design. In an article on global projects entitled 'Team heat' in *CIO Magazine* (1 September 1998), the author reports a consultant's advice:

> Just as you have to recognize the differences between computer operating systems when building a network, so, too, do you need to acknowledge and accommodate the differences between individual team members. He advises CIOs to apply the same rigor to team building as they do to designing any IT project they undertake for the corporation. 'Why,' he asks, 'do we think it's natural to invest millions of dollars to get computer systems to work together, yet we think it's unnatural to invest even a fraction of that cost in designing and educating teams on how to work together?'

So a firm recommendation for international CRM projects is to ensure that – other skill sets being equal – as many key people as possible have had some meaningful international experience during their career, ie that they have actually lived in another country for at least a year. Barring that, then at least ensure that some team members have been part of international projects before.

What you certainly want to avoid ending up with is the real-world example of a US multinational whose corporate IT department at HQ is staffed almost exclusively with people who haven't worked abroad and whose idea of foreign business awareness is knowing that date fields in the rest of the world are written day/month/year. An international project manager at this company simplistically viewed Europe as a more or less homogeneous entity in terms of requirements, and was surprised to discover on his first trip over that there were important variations in some countries because of different legal requirements.

For a list of recommended books, see 'Further reading'.

CHAPTER SUMMARY

▌ International projects are inherently risky, and present an entirely new set of challenges to the project manager. The deck is stacked against such projects, for organizational and cultural reasons.

▌ International CRM projects can only really be justified if the customer base and/or the service being sold are cross-border, which requires data sharing at transactional (as opposed to reporting) level.

▌ Experience shows that standard international processes, especially in the front-office environment of CRM, are unrealistic and generally unachievable.

▌ Ditto for reduced costs through economies of scale and the elimination of duplicate effort, which experience has also shown to be unrealistic and generally unachievable.

▌ International reporting should be viewed as a very desirable by-product of a CRM project, or a secondary driver, but certainly not the main driver.

▌ Successful international project management means taking into account the following critical success factors:

- successfully managing HQ/country relations;
- not letting HQ have 'free' access to country data;
- limiting the number of international software versions;
- keeping the initial architecture simple;
- ensuring that user training is in the local language;
- ensuring that level one support is in the local language;
- ensuring that key project people have international experience.

9

A pilot for proof-of-concept and buy-in

Better to understand a little, than to misunderstand a lot.

(Anonymous)

WHY A PILOT IS AN ABSOLUTE PREREQUISITE

One of the most basic prerequisites for a successful CRM project is an operational pilot, ie one in which the proposed CRM system is actually used in a live environment by selected users for a duration of at least two to three months. There are two main objectives for an operational pilot: 1) to be able to validate the business objectives, and identify and correct the real-world problems that only show up when used in a live environment; 2) to give the project team a chance of getting the users on board by making them feel that they have some power to influence the shape of the finished project. Such early buy-in is essential when the impact on people and process is far-reaching.

There is a school of thought that says that pilots have a downside, in that they get the company mired down in organizational navel-gazing, with the attendant risk of not getting anything out of the door at all. What the no-pilot school is essentially saying is that, by more or less imposing an approach in terms of processes and systems, the users will have no alternative but to bite the bullet and move forward, and that any opposition to change can be dealt with. This is unrealistic.

Another argument against a pilot is that 'double entry', ie entering the same information into two systems, will mean more cost and delay. Indeed, running a pilot for, say, an accounting system might mean double entry because of the requirement for rigorous reporting or integration standards. Fortunately this is not the case for CRM, since it is often easy to segregate a part of the sales force and move them on to a pilot system, provided inputs (products, leads etc) and outputs (orders etc) can be handled seamlessly.

WHY A PILOT IS ESSENTIAL FOR THE SALES FORCE

The requirement for a CRM pilot is essential for the sales force for two main reasons. Firstly, CRM is usually new for the sales force. Traditionally automated functions like order entry, customer service, finance etc have had the time to stabilize process-wise over the past 20–30 years. Even though a pilot would always be beneficial even today for such projects, it would be an exaggeration to say it is indispensable for success. CRM, however, is a totally new area, for which the majority of users – the sales force – are new to automation. SFA is less than 10 years old (except for the pharmaceutical industry, which was the pioneer from as early as the mid-80s). When you're streamlining processes and automating in a functional area for the first time, by definition you're not sure of what to expect. Therefore it makes sense to pilot.

The second reason is that CRM is ultimately 'discretionary' for the sales force. Users in the traditionally automated functions mentioned above have no option but to use whatever system is being proposed – or rather imposed. At the level of Joe or Jane User in such functional areas, you don't usually propose anything; you install and then train people for the new procedures, which are not open for discussion. As long as the new system functions and gets the job done, then people will end up using it. Whether they like it or not is hardly the question. They have to use it, because the previous system has been unplugged, and without a system they cannot do their jobs.

For the sales force, however, which constitutes the main group of CRM users, using a new system is ultimately 'discretionary'. Why? Because they've always worked without a system for their functional area (personal databases like Access, Filemaker Pro, Excel etc don't count, as these remain personal tools fully under their control). Their job is to sell and make their numbers; how they do it is secondary. They might not do it very efficiently in terms of throughput, or even very effectively in terms of doing the right things, but that's not what they're measured against; only the sales numbers count.

So any new system for a sales force is by definition a radical change to the way they work. Regardless of the value proposition of the CRM system for the sales force (the customer, productivity, company reporting etc), there is theoretically nothing to stop them from making their numbers the way they've always been doing before the project came along.

Let's face it, somewhere in the organization almost every month there will be a potential break point when salespeople are justifying why they didn't make their numbers, and the first candidate for abuse will be the system (especially an international one perceived as having been imposed from HQ – see page 96), because it took too long to update the records, because it wouldn't let them do what the customer wanted or any one of a thousand other minor gripes. Sales commission plans don't include big bonuses for 'achieved 100 per cent compliance with the CRM software process manual'. And we all know why salespeople get out of bed in the morning. And it isn't remotely connected to using a CRM system.

For sales reps to be motivated to use a new system, they therefore have to be able to answer the very self-centred question, 'What's in it for me?', ie they want to know if it will help them work more effectively so that they can sell more or sell better. If they cannot, and are therefore unable or unwilling to use the new system, all they have to do is tell the sales manager that it is not helping them to sell and they won't make their numbers if forced to use it. Now, as sales managers are rarely part of a concerted buy-in effort (see Chapter 10), the vast majority will bow to common sense and say something along the lines of, 'OK, I can't force you. Just go and make your numbers – but at least make an effort to learn the new system when you have some time, will you?' In such a situation, the only logical thing to do is to get the buy-in of the sales force, and only a pilot will enable you to see factually whether they can actually benefit from the new system – or if process or system changes are going to be required to make this happen.

HOW LONG SHOULD A PILOT RUN?

A pilot should ideally run for two to three months. Anything less will yield insufficient results, as it usually takes around one month to sort out the inevitable technical glitches and for users to settle down with a new system. Token one-month pilots, usually conceded under pressure or as a sop to 'best practice', are hardly likely to yield usable results and are therefore a waste of everybody's time. Such 'pseudo-pilots' (next section) are ultimately phased implementations, since the clear implication is that whatever happens during the one-month period is not going to change the rest of the project schedule.

KEEP IT SMALL ENOUGH FOR FAILURE TO BE 'ACCEPTABLE'

Many projects start off as either a big-bang implementation, or as a pseudo-pilot, ie a first phase with no option for backtracking. Such projects stand a high chance of ending up in damage-control mode from day one, and then either fail outright or are suitably descoped in order to meet deadlines, regardless of the usefulness of the deliverables. When this happens, the chances are it will be someone else's fault (the vendors, the consultants, the users, IT – take your pick) instead of it simply being a healthy learning experience in a new area.

To gauge if your pilot is small enough, try to answer the following questions. If initially the pilot does not sufficiently validate the expected business objectives and/or if real-world operational problems remain unresolved, then: 1) would it be financially acceptable to say that the amount of money spent was 'small enough' to be written off as an investment in terms of experience and lessons learnt? 2) would it be politically acceptable for the project team to halt or suspend the pilot, and draw on the experience and lessons learnt without heads necessarily rolling?

If you're unable to answer 'yes' to both these questions, then your pilot is either too big (see next section) or is really not a pilot at all but an implicit first phase of the rest of the project.

Some people might argue that this is unrealistic, and that if you could actually have 'acceptable' pilot failure then the original benefits were probably too small in the first place. Well, there are some benefits that might be considered 'small' in absolute terms, but without these basics in place bigger benefits are more difficult to achieve. For example, getting sales and marketing to work together from a shared customer database or getting the sales force to agree to a standard sales funnel is an essential prerequisite for any further process integration across the customer life cycle. The business benefit of a pilot should therefore not be considered as an end in itself but rather as a means to define the way forward.

KEEP SCOPE AND OBJECTIVES BASIC TO ENSURE RAPID RESULTS

Following on from the previous point, if you want to keep your pilot small you necessarily want to keep the scope and objectives basic enough to be able to deliver concrete results in a short time, three to four months maximum. In CRM projects, speed is of the essence, so apply the KISS approach: keep it small and simple. Or alternatively keep it SMART, ie:

- S – specific;
- M – measurable;
- A – actionable;
- R – realistic;
- T – timely.

Building up a project team from the business and IT, and then winning their hearts and minds, can take time. It is therefore important to keep the momentum and deliver results quickly, so people don't have time to doubt. Remember, most ambitious IT projects either fail or fall far short of expectations – so they've heard it all before and only rapid results will ensure you win them over.

Once you've identified your main requirements, prioritize them based on how useful the deliverables would be in building up momentum for the rest of the project and not on how important they are in absolute terms. What this usually translates to in a CRM package is stripping out 50 per cent or more of the myriad of features usually present in the out-of-the-box version. Faced with all that functionality, it is tempting for the business to want to include a bit of this and bit of that for the pilot, and before you know it you've got scope creep.

For example, if the first deliverables are for the sales force that has no prior experience of automation, then simply getting them to adapt to new processes based on a shared customer and opportunity database will be a great achievement. In such a case it is better to stick with the most basic customer profiling and opportunity information, and strip out all the other bells and whistles. It is better for people to get used to something simple and ask for more features than to be overwhelmed by a grand design.

An example of basic scope and objectives for a pilot would be simply to allow the sales force to work on a shared prospect/customer database. Even this basic objective would result in a quantum leap forward in process efficiency and sales effectiveness.

Let's take a very basic example of a sales rep faced with a new lead for Acme Nuts and Bolts. The first thing the rep needs to know is whether Acme is already a customer, in which case it belongs to another sales rep and he or she shouldn't waste another minute on it. If Acme is not a customer, then it's technically a prospect, and the rep should be able to start calling it up – but maybe not, because it could be another sales rep's prospect and the other rep has either already called Acme up or is about to. Or maybe marketing has already targeted Acme with a campaign and is working on the response? So the rep has to be careful not to break into someone else's territory and possibly blow a potential deal someone else is working on. In a non-automated environment, the rep therefore has a lot of non-value-added work to do: e-mails and phone calls to colleagues, sales assistants, marketing or even finance, to find out just what the status of Acme is and whether there's any chance of getting it into his or her portfolio and going after it. Estimated admin time for just this one account: around 10 minutes. Actual lead time in terms of getting replies from all these parties: three to five days. Now multiply this by five new leads per day and you have at least one hour per day of totally non-value-added work before even calling up a prospective customer.

In an automated environment, the rep could query on the shared account database to find out whether Acme is present or not. If it is in the database, the rep would have all the answers right there on the screen, eg it's a customer or it's a prospect, but it's currently being worked on by Jane Doe. Total admin time for this exercise: less than a minute. And all you're really looking at is a shared database of the contact manager kind.

So concentrate on delivering such tangible benefits for a pilot first. This will enable your users to test the usability of the product, and also allow you to base product evolution on actual usage rather than a grand design. As you address more and more business objectives, you can start enabling the bells and whistles of whatever CRM solution you're using.

LEAVE INTEGRATION OUT OF A PILOT

Integration in the form of interfaces to dissimilar systems (eg from sales to order management, or from order management to billing) should not be part of a pilot. The dangers of cross-functional deliverables were already covered in detail in Chapter 6. If it's not recommended for the first phase of a project, it is even less recommended for a pilot. Leave integration for a later phase (granted in some sectors this might not be possible, eg banking and insurance).

BE FLEXIBLE ABOUT WHETHER TO DO UAT

Traditional IT departments with little or no knowledge of software packages, and whose main project experience is with process-driven back-office systems, always have a final project milestone called 'User Acceptance Testing' (UAT). As its name implies, this is supposed to be the ultimate guarantee that whatever's being delivered will actually work in the real world, and is 'contractually' accepted by the business.

Though UAT makes complete sense for projects with systems deliverables, it is nonetheless dependent on the existence of documented processes – of the type readily found in traditional back-office areas, eg a step-by-step process flow for entering an order or fielding a customer call. In the non-automated sales and marketing functions, however, characterized by process immaturity (see

Chapter 3), there are usually no processes as such, much less documented ones, so just how are you supposed to do a UAT? Based on what test scenarios?

So for sales and marketing functions at least, you can't do UAT in the traditional sense. And yet, you have to install the system, and it's going to be used by the business. The solution is to be flexible, remove the 'T' and settle for 'UA', ie general user acceptance of the proposed solution after a demonstration by the project team that it can actually do the processes required at a high level. The training will be based on these high-level processes anyway. Whatever lower-level process steps are used at this stage is irrelevant – usage and gradual adoption will over time result in some form of standardization, which can then be part of a more traditional UAT for successive versions.

Let's take a simple example of the process to update a customer account after a meeting between the sales rep and the customer contact. The end point of this process is an activity against this account showing the meeting date, customer contact person(s) and the objective and outcome of the meeting. How the various preceding sub-processes are handled will vary depending on the individual sales rep. One person might, for example, use the integrated calendar feature and log the telephone call fixing the meeting date, and update it after the meeting. Another rep might use a diary or palm pilot to note the meeting date, and only enter the meeting in the CRM system afterwards. The end result is the same, and at this stage of the project you should not bother with the detailed process steps of the type usually associated with UAT.

In conclusion, therefore, don't get hung up with UAT for a pilot, especially one that covers the sales and/or marketing functions. If it's good enough, ship it. Leave UAT for a later phase when processes are stable enough to be documented and agreed by all.

HOW TO CHOOSE A PILOT GROUP, SITE OR COUNTRY

As the objective for a pilot is to validate business objectives and to identify and resolve potential operational problems, you'll want to choose a pilot group, site or country with an environment that does not interfere with these objectives. This is best explained via some examples:

▌ If a site is relocating to a new building just before the pilot date, then your pilot stands every chance of being disrupted by technical incidents and the sudden unavailability of people, both from the business and from IT.

▌ If the site chosen for a pilot is characterized by well-known data quality issues, then the resolution of this problem suddenly becomes a prerequisite for the pilot. In a worst-case scenario, it can take so long that it becomes a data migration project in its own right (see page 83).

▌ If a regional office or country has serious organizational issues at senior management or executive level for whatever reason, then any resulting turbulence or fallout could disrupt the pilot.

In all these examples, a problem that at the outset has no direct relation to CRM and your pilot objectives now all of a sudden becomes part and parcel of the pilot. From the business sponsor's point of view, it's now all one and the same, ie if these 'external' factors seriously impact the pilot, it will be difficult to separate the problem from CRM and say that in its absence the pilot can be shown to be a success.

You should therefore choose your pilot group, site or country using the following guidelines:

▌ large enough to be representative of the rest of the company, but not so large that political and organizational issues start to overshadow the pilot;

▌ has been operating for at least two years, to guarantee a sufficient level of process maturity (regardless of whether those processes are documented or not);

▌ a central office location, rather than one or more regional sites, to reduce bandwidth and connectivity issues, and to reduce the chances of a lengthy, multiple-site data migration effort;

▌ one with the fewest data quality problems, which will result in the easiest data migration effort, eg a sales organization with a shared customer/prospect database, and/or one with standard Excel templates;

▌ online users only, ie no offline usage requiring database synchronization (see page 161);

▌ for an international project, a country that is large enough in terms of sales to be representative, but not so large that the business risk of a full roll-out becomes unacceptable in the case of failure.

This should ensure that the pilot remains focused on functionality, proof-of-concept and demonstrable business benefits, and is not disrupted or bogged down by peripheral issues that have little or nothing to do with what you are trying to achieve.

LIMIT AN INTERNATIONAL PILOT TO A SINGLE COUNTRY

For an international CRM pilot, the question arises as to whether to get input from all countries or to keep a pilot focused on one country only and then throw it open to the rest afterwards. The clear advantage of getting input from all countries for a pilot is that the end result will be much more representative. However, there are two disadvantages that nonetheless make this a risky proposition: 1) There's no such thing as a homogeneous international entity. Different countries are necessarily at different maturity levels; they will therefore have different marginal requirements and different priorities. 2) The more entities, business units or countries you have designing something, the greater the risk of being bogged down in politics, turf and organizational issues, with each trying to out-process the other in an attempt to get the pilot to reflect their particular way of working.

So the clear recommendation is for the project team to select one country for the pilot (based on the criteria in the previous section) and, once this is considered a success, get agreement from the rest of the world for the next phase. This is achieved by holding an international pilot validation workshop, in the form of a one- or two-day session attended by a cross-section of senior management and users from all countries. The objective of this workshop is to obtain country buy-in at senior management level. However, that's not sufficient; just because a country's sales director says, 'Let's do it' doesn't necessarily mean the troops agree. You therefore need to follow this up with an international road show to obtain buy-in at user level. Case study 3 (Chapter 13) shows a real-world example of an international CRM project with a pilot limited to one country, followed by a pilot validation workshop and then an international road show.

CHAPTER SUMMARY

▮ An operational pilot is essential to be able to validate business objectives, and identify and correct the real-world problems that only show up when used in a live environment.

▮ A pilot is essential for the sales force because: 1) CRM is usually new, unlike the traditionally automated functions like order entry, finance etc; 2) a CRM tool is ultimately 'discretionary', ie salespeople won't be forced to use it if they can convince their boss that it will affect their sales.

▮ A pilot should run for at least two to three months. Anything less will yield insufficient results, as it usually takes around one month to sort out the inevitable technical glitches and for users to settle down with a new system.

▮ The scope of a pilot should be small enough for failure to be 'acceptable'. The business benefits of a pilot should not be considered as ends in themselves, but rather as a means to define the way forward.

▮ Keep the scope and objectives of a pilot basic enough to be able to deliver concrete results in a short time, three to four months maximum. It is important to keep the momentum and deliver results quickly, so people don't have time to doubt (remember, they've heard it all before).

▮ Integration in the form of interfaces to other systems should not be part of a pilot, because of the technical complexities and the risks associated with cross-functional deliverables.

▮ Don't get hung up with UAT for a pilot, especially one that covers the sales and/or marketing functions. If it's good enough and has been accepted, ship it. Leave UAT for a later phase when processes are stable enough to be documented and agreed by all.

▮ A pilot group, site or country should be chosen in such a way that the pilot remains focused on functionality, proof-of-concept and demonstrable business benefits, and is not disrupted or bogged down by peripheral issues that have little or nothing to do with what you are trying to achieve.

▌ Limit an international pilot to one country, because of the different maturity levels of each country and the risk of organizational politics. You can get agreement from the rest of the world after a successful pilot in one country.

10

Buy-in from sales managers

When you've got them by their wallets, their hearts and
minds will follow.
(Fern Naito, quoted in MacHale, 1997)

WHY SALES MANAGER BUY-IN IS ESSENTIAL

When discussing why a pilot is an absolute prerequisite (see
Chapter 9), we saw that the main users – the sales reps – are in the
enviable position of being able to 'decide' whether they will actually use a CRM system or not. This means that there must be a clear
focus by the project team on providing tangible benefits for this key
population of users, who can make or break a CRM project.

However, there is another key group of users – maybe even more
important than the sales reps – and that is their sales managers. The
most common organizational structure in sales is to have sales reps
reporting to sales managers, who in turn report to a sales director.
The sales director has sales targets, which are broken down
amongst the sales managers, who are in charge of a particular territory. Sales managers are therefore responsible for territory plans, ie
account segmentation and territory assignments for their sales reps.

They are the managers and coaches of their sales reps to ensure they meet their objectives.

In order to do all of this effectively, sales managers need constant information from the reps on their leads, their active prospects and the progress of their opportunities. A CRM tool is extremely well positioned to provide this information, and can make sales managers much more effective. In fact, of all the groups in the sales organization, sales managers probably derive the most benefit from the use of a CRM or SFA tool.

This means that your best allies in the battle for mind share and buy-in in a CRM project are the sales managers. Of course this is contingent upon buy-in from the sales director, but he or she can only provide leadership and sell the vision. However, actually implementing those changes in terms of buy-in to processes and systems can best come from the sales managers.

The close relationship sales managers have with their teams means they are *the* best people to sell the reps on the benefits of a CRM system – not even the sales director or a VP could do it better. Sales managers also have the key advantage of being able to lay the ground rules for mandatory usage – and to get compliance, something that the rest of the organization is unable to do. In short, if someone has to wield the stick, sales managers are the ones who have the best chance of doing it effectively.

HOW SALES MANAGERS CAN MAKE OR BREAK A PROJECT

When it comes to CRM, sales managers can wield tremendous influence over their sales reps, both positive and negative. On the positive side, sales managers can be instrumental during the training session in helping their reps to buy into the new processes and benefits, and help to answer the famous question, 'What's in it for me?' After their teams have been trained, they can also insist that all reporting and activity management should now be done using the new system, ie they will no longer rely on e-mail or attachments. In weekly meetings, for example, or one-to-one sessions with sales reps, if reps refer to leads or ongoing opportunities and haven't entered it in the system, all sales managers have to say is that the leads are not visible on their laptops and they won't talk about them till they are. You can be reasonably sure that, within one week of training, all the team will be using the new system. Of course, sales managers need to be motivated to take this line (next section).

On the negative side, sales managers can do exactly the opposite – with devastating results. Here are two real-world examples. 1) During an SFA training session in Case study 2 (Chapter 13), sales managers categorically rejected the new system, with comments like, 'Whoever dreamt up these processes doesn't know how we really work' and, 'We never validated any of this anyway'. 2) On another project, one month into a national roll-out for around 50 regional sales managers and 500 sales reps, I was reviewing the usage statistics by region with someone who'd been at the company for over 20 years and knew just about every sales manager, having worked with them for many years when he himself was in the field. He didn't even have to look at the statistics to be able to identify with startling accuracy those regional managers who were likely to encourage or discourage usage of the new system by their teams ('This one's anti-technology – don't hold your breath', 'This one couldn't care less as long as he makes his numbers', 'This one created an Access database, so you can expect good usage here', etc).

As the ratio of sales managers to sales reps is around one to eight, you can see that you don't need more than a handful of sales managers to send an implicit or explicit message of non-coopera-tion to their teams, effectively stalling the project.

HOW TO ACHIEVE BUY-IN FROM SALES MANAGERS

So now that we're all convinced that getting sales manager buy-in is a critical success factor, how can we achieve it? The basic prerequi-site is an operational pilot with full participation of a sales manager and that manager's team. Enough has been said about the impor-tance of a pilot (see Chapter 9).

After a successful pilot (which should by definition yield at least one enthusiastic sales manager), the roll-out for the rest of the project should include the following key activities and milestones:

▌ Hold a one-day off-site workshop for all sales managers (have multiple workshops for a large sales force – you don't want more than eight sales managers in a session), with the objective of selling the product and the benefits of the new/changed processes. This workshop would be run by the project team, mainly the project owner and project manager, with the full participation of the sales manager for the pilot. This group will demonstrate the pilot product to the rest of the sales force, emphasizing the lessons learnt during the pilot and quantifying wherever possible the benefits and areas of concern. This should then be followed by a mini-training hands-on session, so that they can get a feel for the new tool. Open debate about the pros and cons of this type of project should be encouraged; it is important to get all the issues on the table for an informed decision. At the end of the workshop, there should be a vote on how to proceed, based on factual benefits and real concerns. Needless to say, a whole day taken out of the sales managers' selling time can only be obtained with the full blessing and buy-in of the sales director, whose presence should in any case be mandatory.

▌ The feedback from this workshop should condition the actual roll-out. If the sales managers are not sold on the benefits of the solution, for whatever reason, why proceed with a roll-out to sales reps who will take their cue from their sales managers?

▌ Sales managers must be present at the training sessions for their teams. The fact that they already attended the workshop must under no circumstances be an excuse not to attend the training session with their teams. Their role during their teams' training is essential: they are there to anticipate objections, placate Luddites, ensure process buy-in – and especially make it abundantly clear throughout the session that as from the very next day the only channel of communication for reporting will be the new system.

▌ For sales managers to expose themselves in this way by wielding the stick and laying their credibility on the line with respect to their team requires a reliable product, reliable data and very extensive support during the first few weeks. If any of these key requirements are perceived as being inadequate, even the most well-intentioned sales manager might defect and fall back to the old ways – with disastrous results, because you won't get a second chance for such cooperation. So the project plan should also include these three key go/no-go milestones to roll-out: a reliable product, quality data and adequate support.

In conclusion, major battles are won by choosing your allies wisely. Sales managers are the best allies for a CRM project when it comes to actual end users. Get them all bought in and you're 80 per cent there, at least as far as the sales force is concerned. If you don't have this buy-in – and by this I don't mean just 'signed-off' buy-in, but enthusiastic and palpable buy-in – you might as well put the project on hold. If not bought into the project and its benefits, sales managers have the potential to stop any CRM initiative by labelling it, rightly or wrongly, as impacting their sales – and there won't be much the sales director can do about it.

Sales directors who meet or exceed their numbers but aren't very hot on the new CRM project will get away with a slap on the wrist. If, however, they do not make their numbers, their enthusiasm for the CRM project is not going to be of much help in getting them out of trouble. And sales managers are the key to making the numbers. Sales directors will therefore take very seriously whatever the managers say about the new CRM solution.

CHAPTER SUMMARY

▌ Getting buy-in from sales managers should be an explicit part of a CRM project because of their influence in the sales organization, both with respect to the sales director and with respect to their sales reps. It doesn't take more than a handful of 'uncooperative' sales managers to stall a CRM project.

▌ Sales manager buy-in should be obtained in a special one-day, off-site meeting, with the explicit objective of obtaining a green light from them for the rest of the project.

▌ The presence of sales managers at their teams' training sessions should be mandatory. Their role is to anticipate objections, placate Luddites and ensure process buy-in for their teams.

Part III

Risk factors for CRM

11

Risk factors

Good judgement comes from bad experience, and a lot of that
comes from bad judgement.

(Anonymous, from the quotes archive on www.jokes2go.com)

ORGANIZATIONAL CHANGE AND COMPANY POLITICS

Companies don't start CRM projects; people do. These dynamic
visionaries, usually charismatic and forward-thinking executives,
are often the key to initiating CRM, whether tactical or strategic.
The more strategic and all-embracing the initiative, however, the
more important it is for it to be supported by multiple executives.
However, the reality of company politics means they are usually
unable or unwilling to find allies at executive level.

Except in the extremely rare cases when CRM is launched by the
CEO, CRM projects are therefore usually associated with a single
executive, who has the awesome responsibility of carrying the
project through to completion. Even when there is an executive
steering committee, there's no doubt as to whose project it is. This
implicit one-person-show, however, carries the danger of the
project being jeopardized if for whatever reason this person leaves,

usually after the umpteenth executive reorganization. The initiative then stands a good chance of dying a natural death, and might never be resurrected, at least not in the same form. After all, a newly arrived executive is hardly going to stand up and endorse a predecessor's incomplete project!

Key projects like CRM hardly ever fail because of a critical mass of opposition; they fail because of a lack of allies in high places. This organizational reality is part of the landscape and, since it cannot be changed, you have to try to limit this risk factor as far as possible. And the best way to do that is to deliver business benefit quickly to ensure credibility: the quicker there are tangible deliverables that can then become institutionalized, the harder it will be for organizational politics to dislodge them once an executive sponsor moves on.

The more strategic and ambitious a CRM project, the longer will be the lead time for tangible deliverables, and consequently the more exposed the project will be to organizational change and company politics. So to limit this risk factor, break down your large-scale CRM vision into sufficiently small tactical initiatives with a life cycle that is well inside the half-life of the average executive's time in office.

TOO MANY CONSULTANTS, TOO FEW IN-HOUSE STAFF

Once you've selected a CRM solution, you can't just sign a blank cheque to a systems integrator or a big-X consulting firm, and expect them to do the job. While integrators and consultants can and do deliver value, the client has a huge responsibility for creating and sustaining the conditions under which this will occur. At best this is seriously underestimated by the client, and at worst totally ignored. The result is that most CRM projects are heavily dependent on consultants and integrators, to the detriment of knowledgeable permanent staff.

Many companies often simplistically view CRM as primarily a one-time, technical/product-related effort, which can therefore be outsourced. In reality, however, it is as much functional as technical, and real-world functional knowledge lies in-house. It is also far from one-time, so both the functional and the technical resources will be needed for many years down the road.

The experiences of ERP over the past 10 years have no doubt influenced this. ERP is essentially a big-bang implementation, resulting in a relatively process-stable environment with the company taking up the slack after the consultants have packed their bags and left. CRM, however, is long-term, multi-module, cross-functional and ever changing, in order to cope with a front-office environment in constant flux. If the required resources are mainly outsourced via an integrator and consultants, then the cycle time and the costs of losing knowledgeable resources, and having new ones learn the business and the customized solution all over again, become prohibitive. You therefore need an in-house centre of excellence that is in it for the long haul. Crucial business knowledge must be retained by business analysts, and technical staff should be able to bring out new versions of the product rapidly.

A simple example is the difficulty of capturing and retaining business requirements from senior management and from actual users, all of whom have jobs to do and usually don't have the time to come to meetings. When such meetings do take place – often by decree – the chances of getting the same group of people together a second time are extremely slim. The knowledge imparted during such meetings and sessions is of such vital importance for the project that it absolutely must be captured by permanent staff. To have it going mainly or exclusively to consultants who won't be around three months later (when it will inevitably be needed again) represents an enormous waste of time and money. The factual meeting minutes documented by the consultants for future use will not be able to portray the non-verbal elements that at the end of the day are more important than what was actually said. For those interested, research shows that the message that comes across when people speak is only 10 per cent related to the actual words they say, with the remaining 90 per cent coming from their tone of voice and body language.

Here is another example, this time on the technical side. CRM products are normally configured or developed in an iterative manner, with direct feedback from the business to the developers during workshops. Developers consequently end up acquiring detailed knowledge of the ins and outs of the business, and thus become exponentially more productive over time, which makes them more valuable to retain. It makes sense for such people to be part of the client's organization rather than the integrator's organization.

The bottom line therefore is that you must have your own staff to work alongside your integrator and consultants to ensure that knowledge is retained: 1) Business analysts are an absolute must – this is by far the most important, as mentioned above. 2) The level of technical staff needed for CRM product configuration is dependent on the degree of deviation from the standard, out-of-the-box version, and the rate of change of your business requirements. The more you customize the product and the faster your requirements change, the more you will require new versions and the greater will be your need to retain technical knowledge in-house. The company in Case study 3 (Chapter 13) followed this approach; in a triple-digit, high-growth, international environment with new products, new countries and reorganizations every few months, it would have proved impossible for the traditional integrator/consultant approach to keep pace.

Not surprisingly, integrators prefer to work with only their own teams, and don't look too kindly on customers wanting to have their own resources working alongside them. So work out a deal with the integrator up front to ensure that a learning process and skills transfer to your own staff is part of the contract.

The alternative is to set up your own centre of excellence, with permanent staff in all key positions to manage the project and produce the deliverables, and fill the remaining gap with contractors or consultants (see Case study 3, Chapter 13). Unlike the big-X integrators, there are many smaller consulting companies that are more than willing to provide between one and five people to work under the responsibility of the client. It's a win situation for them, as they get valuable experience and the benefit of the reference.

In conclusion, don't look at CRM as a one-time, technical effort you can outsource – the lack of business and technical expertise will come back to haunt you right after implementation. Build up your in-house organization to include permanent staff to ensure knowledge is retained and your CRM project can grow using the same people.

IT RESISTANCE TO ORGANIZATIONAL CHANGE

Resisting organizational change is usually seen on the business side, as it comes to grips with the realities of CRM. However, the same phenomenon can be observed in some IT departments.

The structure of the traditional IT organization in large companies is incompatible with CRM. Naturally reflecting the internal business customers it serves under the non-CRM model, IT is structured by vertical function, eg a silo for sales, another for order entry, another for customer service etc, each responsible for a vertical system and each dealing exclusively with its part of the business.

Dialogue between these different IT departments is confined essentially to interfacing requirements, as in, 'Tell me what you need from my system and I'll tell you if I have it'. This interface approach was essentially for efficiency reasons, eg eliminating duplicate data entry, eliminating order rejection rate etc. It was rarely for CRM-related reasons, eg being able to view a customer from an enterprise perspective for increased sales or better customer service. This function-based approach explains why there are so many stovepipe systems in the same company, each with its own narrowly focused view of the world, and characterized by duplicate and often incompatible customer data.

As a customer-facing function, however, CRM requires an IT organization with a horizontal component. It is no longer sufficient for separate IT groups to talk to their respective business customers, and then get together after the fact to try to tie it all together in terms of interfaces. CRM is not about interfaces for efficiency reasons; it's about providing a coherent cross-functional view of the customer. You therefore need a group of people from IT representing processes rather than functions, talking to all of the business at the same time, with the customer as the common thread.

This is easier said than done; any such horizontal group would cut across the traditional boundaries and fiefdoms of the traditional IT organization. This could lead to IT being biased more towards a CRM approach that favours its traditional organizational structure rather than the requirements of the business. For example, architecturally it might favour separate vertical systems for each function with interfaces to each other, instead of a single, horizontal application serving multiple functions. This delays the difficult decision of deciding which IT silo, sales or service (or a new entity) now becomes top dog. The following example shows just how such organizational resistance impacted a major CRM project.

At one multinational, a successful implementation of a leading CRM solution for sales and marketing led to the business requirement to extend this customer-centric approach through to order management for a newly launched product. But instead of being viewed as a natural extension of the sales and marketing project run by the IT manager for sales and marketing, it was handled as a separate project by the IT manager for customer service, whose responsibilities covered order management systems. Unfortunately, his team had no experience of the CRM vendor's product, since the current order management system was a stovepipe based on an in-house-developed system. So with the business pressure to get started, a compromise was reached whereby the customer service IT manager now in charge of the project would use the sales and marketing IT manager as an internal subcontractor. His CRM centre of excellence, which did the initial implementation, would extend the existing sales and marketing solution by incorporating order entry and order management features.

The customer service IT manager had no experience of either CRM or packaged solutions, so he adopted the traditional 'waterfall' method with its exhaustive requirements approach (see the following section). The CRM centre of excellence, however, didn't work this way, and used the prototype-based, workshop approach normally associated with CRM packages. So the pilot ended up being unofficially managed by the sales and marketing IT manager's CRM centre of excellence, with the customer service IT manager's group effectively reduced to a spectator role.

In five months the pilot was completed, and successfully installed in one country. For the very first time in the company's history, there was order flow-through from sales to service in a single CRM system with a single customer database (albeit for a single product). Within a few months this country was able to report significant benefits, mainly the streamlining of processes between sales and service, and a 30 per cent reduction in order cycle time.

The IT organization now had a window of opportunity to build upon this successful pilot and reorganize or merge the two managers' groups along CRM lines. Alas, internal politics and organizational turf got the upper hand. The pilot was stopped, and there was to be no further roll-out or any further enhancements. Traditional organizational boundaries meant that any project that targeted order management was the preserve of the customer service IT manager, and the fact that the sales and marketing IT manager had pulled off a successful pilot was to be treated as an experiment for proof-of-concept.

The customer service IT manager then put together a project plan that called for training his existing team on the CRM vendor's product, bringing in new people and delivering an order management system with at least the same functionality as the pilot – all within the space of five months. In other words, a team with no knowledge of either CRM or the CRM vendor's product was going to take five months from the word go to build a better system than a very experienced CRM centre of excellence! Amazingly, IT actually sold this vision to the international business. Only the CRM centre of excellence saw it as totally unrealistic and inspired almost exclusively by questions of organizational turf.

But there was more – instead of having a single instance of the CRM product spanning both sales and service, with shared data and shared development, each IT group would continue to operate independently and deliver two separate instances of the same CRM product: one for sales and one for service, with duplicate customer and order data, and a traditional interface to pass the order from sales to service!

And finally, as if the deck wasn't already sufficiently stacked against the project, a third person, the programme manager in charge of integrating these sales and service projects, also worked with the traditional waterfall approach. He produced a 200-plus page statement of requirements comprising over 300 separate high-level 'requirements', duly 'signed off' by the business – and more or less unusable by either the sales or the service IT teams.

Of course, the inevitable happened, and the original five-month deadline stretched to eight months and then to a year. IT – now pressured by the business for results – threw in the towel after 15 months and many millions of dollars. After a major IT reorganization in which some key heads rolled (and not just because of this project – there was unfortunately another failed CRM initiative), the original pilot of one year earlier was resurrected for two countries that needed it badly, and the CIO ordered the creation of a horizontal CRM group spanning both sales and service. On the architecture side, the recommendation of this new group was not two but a single instance of the CRM product for both sales and services, with full data sharing and a single development environment.

The above example might seem extreme, but it happened in a large, brand-name multinational with operations around the world, and characterized by a large, old-school IT organization. There are many large companies that fit this description.

So how can you ensure that IT resistance to organizational change does not impact a CRM project? The solution lies at CIO level. The various senior directors in charge of sales and customer service are not going spontaneously to give up some of their responsibilities in favour of the other person or in favour of a new horizontal entity. Only the CIO can step in and reorganize appropriately based on the new business requirements centred around CRM.

USING THE WATERFALL APPROACH

You may be surprised to learn that old-school IT departments with minimal experience of off-the-shelf packages have survived into the 21st century. But they do exist. While the rest of the world was evaluating solutions in terms of 'buy or build', they somehow managed to remain wedded to the concept of NIH (not invented here), in which the only valid systems were developed in-house.

Implicit in the classical build approach is the use of the traditional waterfall or 'cascade' method, so called because of the image of water falling over successive phases, each of which is conditioned by approval before being able to proceed with the next one. This rigidly procedural, life-cycle approach starts off with analysts sitting down one-to-one with business users in an attempt to understand requirements, ultimately producing a thick 'requirements' document that nobody, even with the best of intentions, can really fully understand. Once the so-called 'statement of requirements' (SoR) has been duly 'signed off' by the business, IT will then try to build a system to meet those requirements – which may or may not correspond to actual requirements.

While some IT departments use this approach in a genuine attempt to get the business to commit to real as opposed to perceived needs, there are others that unfortunately use it as a contractual safeguard – because, once the business has signed off on an SoR, it means IT can produce a system that addresses the documented requirements and has therefore fulfilled its obligation. If, for whatever reason, the signed-off SoR does not reflect real requirements, then IT can use it as a 'get out of jail free' card, as in Monopoly, and not be penalized. This waterfall approach is largely responsible for IT's legendary woes: high costs, low returns, eternal maintenance, dissatisfied users.

The problem with the waterfall approach is that, like a waterfall, the business is constantly moving. Enormous amounts of energy are expended in defining in detail precisely what is required at the time the requirements are gathered or – if you are lucky – some time between when they were gathered and when the documentation was actually signed (which does not always happen). Then the business moves on and real life intervenes to ensure that at least some of the requirements shift. But the changes never find their way back to the development team, who become obsessed with interpreting the documented requirements like a judge trying to find the 'will of parliament' in the words of legislation, without any concern for what the business needs today or will need by the time the project actually delivers something. Of course if the people in the business have any sense, they make vague mutterings about the completeness of the SoR without actually signing anything ('Sorry, I didn't have time actually to read it all in detail, but it seems fine, so you IT people just get on with building it and I'll get back to you as soon as I can find some time to read it').

The waterfall approach denies three essential realities:

▌ Requirements for many business systems are usually moving targets – this is especially true for CRM because it is so new. Fitting CRM systems to businesses is therefore like fitting shoes to children: 1) you can guarantee that the child will have changed long before the shoes wear out; 2) if you take three to 12 months to build a pair of shoes, you had better get used to bare-footed children.

▌ Committees of users who are supposed to define requirements are like marketing focus groups – they usually follow a reductive approach. They can only tell you whether they like or don't like what you present them with. Have you heard of the focus group that invented the Walkman? Neither have I. It didn't exist because, before some bright spark in Sony invented it, the general public didn't know it could be done or how it would change their lives. So how can you expect a group of users to define requirements in an afternoon if they only discuss process when it involves trying to get people to do something they don't want to do, with a direct impact on their commission? People need to be given a chance to know what the system is capable of and how their colleagues will cope with it before they can define what the real 'requirements' are.

▌ Specifying one's requirements is not something that comes naturally to users. Just ask any five people to write down the 'requirements' for setting the table: you'll get five different answers, and each person will have left something out. So why do we expect users to be able correctly to 'specify' requirements for business subjects many times more complex? In reality, specifying requirements is an iterative process, which requires intermediate results (ie in IT terms, a prototype) for the business to adjust or confirm what they previously thought. For the example of setting a table, by simply looking at a partially set table (a 'prototype'), it will become much more obvious if something is missing (eg salt and pepper, water, serviettes...).

Fortunately, there is another school of thought on methodology that recognizes this reality. Whatever the various permutations and their names, eg joint application design (JAD), rapid application development (RAD), process workshops etc, they all subscribe to the following basic premises:

▌ You can only gather proper requirements when all players are around the same table discussing the issues from a horizontal, company perspective, rather than a vertical, departmental perspective.

▌ Such requirements are obtained in interactive workshop sessions rather than one-to-one interviews or meetings.

▌ The resulting requirements are not cast in concrete, but will need to be adjusted and confirmed in a subsequent phase by reviewing an intermediate result, usually in the form of a usable, prototype application.

Such workshop sessions are usually run by two professional consultants, one standing in front picking the users' brains and sticking post-it notes on the wall representing processes and data, and a 'scribe', who notes down all the information. This then becomes part of the documented deliverables, which weigh in at 15–30 pages maximum. This comprises:

▌ formal business definitions (what is a customer, a contract etc, which can sometimes take a day or more to gain consensus on);

▌ high-level processes broken down into lower-level processes (usually one or two levels down), which can then be mapped to similar processes in a CRM package;

▌ optionally, data entities and relationships.

This iterative approach is an established part of virtually all CRM vendors' methodologies, and is adopted by most integrators as well. It is instrumental in making users active participants with a personal stake in the final outcome, instead of passive customers with an eye on the contract.

When old-school IT with its rigid adherence to the waterfall method meets the modern world of packaged CRM solutions, then you have a culture clash and worlds in collision. If the old-school IT department insists on tradition, then you run the almost-certain risk of delaying project deliverables by six months or more:

▌ It will take at least three months for business analysts to produce an SoR of a couple of hundred pages.

▌ It will then take another three months before it becomes politically acceptable to agree that not many people understand it, especially those who have to use it to evaluate candidate solutions and to customize the chosen product to meet these 'requirements'.

▌ You then have to start all over again at square one, which could take another few months, because it is not easy to get the business to agree to a second round of requirements gathering.

This is exactly what happened in the real-world example in the previous section: a couple of hundred pages of incomprehensible 'requirements' took three months to produce, and it was another three months before it was organizationally acceptable to ignore them. By the time 'proper' requirements at last appeared, the project had slipped nine months, whereas the application of the workshop-based iterative method would have yielded usable requirements in a matter or days or weeks at the most.

If you are part of a project that purports to define business requirements as part of the waterfall approach, the only politically acceptable thing is to request outside assistance from either a consulting company or the CRM vendor, or both, so that it can be made abundantly clear to the business sponsor the risks of going down such a route.

AN RFP-BASED PACKAGE SELECTION PROCESS

When old-school IT does opt for buying instead of building, it usually finds itself in a new environment. Not surprisingly, therefore, it ends up adopting a traditional RFP-based approach for package selection.

A logical extension of the first phase of the waterfall approach mentioned above, it takes the supposedly exhaustive SoR and sends it off to a number of CRM vendors, who are then supposed to generate a proposal whose validity will be dependent on the compliance of their product to the 'requirements' listed in the SoR. This then results in a long-drawn-out, bureaucratic process in search of the holy grail, which becomes an end in itself. This usually feeds another long-drawn-out process: the detailed, finicky and minute customization of the chosen product to correspond to the exhaustive requirements stated in the RFP. Though the final deliverable theoretically corresponds to 'requirements', in practice it is often unusable.

Contrary to the traditional RFP approach, CRM requirements (indeed any requirements) should not be exhaustive – they should be limited to critical and important needs. You should consider secondary needs only after you know that a package can meet your critical and important needs. Exhaustive requirements checklists have the following disadvantages:

▌ Preparing them is a time-consuming exercise that can become an end in itself (the term 'exhaustive' doesn't just apply to the requirements themselves).

▌ Instead of focusing on the essentials, user departments tend to 'out-feature' each other to remain visible.

▌ Vendors focus less on the essentials and concentrate instead on meeting as many requirements as possible.

▌ Users tend to defend their requirements as sacred. If a package does not have their pet features, they may not be receptive to other positive things about it, or may fail to see alternative ways of achieving the same results.

▌ Any missing feature automatically becomes part of a list of potential enhancements, even though it may not be that important.

Keep requirements short (no more than 30 pages) and focused on basic processes, so that you can get to the demonstration phase more quickly, which is where the vendors will show you how they address those processes. Short requirements lists also ensure that users and vendors focus on essentials, options remain open and users aren't prematurely locked into positions they feel obliged to defend later – if only to save face. After a couple of demonstrations, users will probably have new ideas about how to handle their secondary requirements.

If you are part of a project that adopts an RFP approach to evaluating and selecting CRM products, then request outside assistance from a consulting company, so that the risks of going down such a route can be made abundantly clear to the business sponsor.

THE COMPLEXITIES OF OFFLINE USAGE WITH SYNCHRONIZATION

How does synchronization work?

Most CRM packages allow remote users (in practice the sales force) to work offline in disconnected mode and connect to the network at their convenience to synchronize with the central database – just like offline e-mail usage, which allows you to work on the plane, for example, and then connect later when you get to your hotel. Offline CRM usage enables users to extract their slice of the database on to their laptop, work offline and connect again to synchronize changes.

Whereas the business benefits of working offline on your e-mail are clear and indisputable (except perhaps to your spouse and kids), the same cannot necessarily be said for offline CRM usage. Except in the case of PDAs, these business benefits are usually exaggerated by the sales force, for whom it is usually a convenience more than anything else. However, the complexity (never mind the costs) and the constraints associated with this mode of working, especially for a large sales force in a highly volatile data environment, can quickly bring a CRM project to its knees.

The constraints of offline usage

Working offline on a laptop is very appealing, because you don't have to be constantly connected. However, like all good features, it can come at a cost:

▮ *Impact on user satisfaction.* In order to limit synchronization times to an acceptable three to five minutes (36–56 kbps modem speeds), users have to synchronize every day. Regardless of policies and procedures, some will do it daily, or every two to three days, or weekly, leading to synchronization times that can vary from minutes to an hour or more depending on account volumes and updates. This will have a direct impact on user satisfaction.

▮ *Inaccurate reporting.* 'What you see isn't always what you get': reporting accuracy from the central database will be a direct function of user adherence to synchronization policies and procedures. The best-case scenario is that once a week at a certain time (eg at cut-off time for weekly reporting) the database will be accurate; the rest of the week no reliable reporting can be produced. Note that this best-case scenario is also theoretical; there are always valid reasons for people not to synchronize when required (illness, other priorities, putting it off for the next day etc). This translates into additional overheads for sales operations when it comes to reporting, because before any central report can be produced someone is going to have to check that every sales rep has indeed synchronized.

▮ *Fluctuating synchronization times.* Synchronization times for users are dependent not only on their own changes to their local database but also on changes made by others in the central database. For example, in a high-volume campaign and lead-generation environment, there can be lots of new or changed data for sales reps initiated by others, ie even if they didn't use the system at all during the day, there could still be lots of updates waiting for them when they next connect. The next day when (if?) they sign on, therefore, they could be surprised it's taking so long, and they might call the help desk.

▮ *A planning process for marketing campaigns.* If such campaign-generated data changes are in volumes sufficient to cause unacceptably high synchronization times, the sales reps would be better off having their databases completely reloaded by IT – which would require them to bring their laptops to the office. This implies introducing a planning process into marketing campaigns to ensure that campaign responses can actually be used by the sales force.

▌ *A planning process for mass updates.* When companies do mass updates (eg reassigning accounts to a different user, address standardization etc), a very rigorous planning process will have to be introduced to ensure that users: 1) synchronize all their changes before the mass update is run; 2) do not change any of their data until the update is run centrally, usually overnight; 3) are informed that their next synchronization will take longer than usual because of the changes. If a user didn't follow these directives and carried on working normally, the next time he or she connected he/she would get a lot of 'collisions', which is when the system detects that the same information has been changed by different users, and one of the changes is rejected.

▌ *A planning process for new versions.* In order to upgrade to a new version, users must synchronize and not use the application before they get the new version. Once again, a planning process with usage constraints needs to be introduced.

▌ *No access to interfaced systems.* An offline user has no access to other systems to which the CRM system might be interfaced, eg viewing the status of an order in a back-office system, or information in the billing system.

None of the above disadvantages apply for users who work online. The inability to work offline is compensated for by the absence of all of the above constraints; the only requirement is a connection with sufficient bandwidth (eg the LAN at the office, and ISDN or ADSL at home).

A real-world example of the difficulties of offline usage

At the telco in Case study 2 (Chapter 13), no level of policies or procedures could enforce the requirement for daily synchronization. The central database was therefore never up to date, and accurate reporting, one of the major drivers for the project, was not possible. This reality was embarrassingly driven home one day during a meeting between the CEO of the package vendor and the CEO of the telco. The IT manager, who was also present, turned on his laptop and proudly displayed a screen of the weekly sales funnel based on a snapshot of the day before. Far from admiring the funnel's colours and vivid graphics, the CEO was more concerned with the forecasting numbers displayed. After a few seconds he said, 'Those figures can't be right!', to which the cornered IT manager could only reply, 'Uh, well, all the sales reps have not yet synchronized the changes on their laptops. This will be done by Wednesday night'. Fortunately for the CEO (and unfortunately for the project), his official sales forecasting came from paper-based reports. Just as well, because the sexy funnel never once showed the correct forecasting numbers.

This telco was also targeting the SME market, which resulted in high-volume campaign updates on a weekly basis (new accounts, updates to existing accounts, new leads). This required a planning process to be introduced in which the sales force was informed by e-mail that, on this or that day of the month, they should expect very high synchronization times and not be alarmed. Since this wasn't treated as urgent mail, it was usually read too late or not read at all, resulting in the help desk being swamped with calls from frustrated users. New-version releases were also very difficult for the same reasons. These process and usage constraints were so great that, six months after going live, the remote features were disabled and everyone was put on mandatory online access.

When offline usage works well

The above issues don't imply that offline usage is to be avoided at all costs, only that it is not an absolute and should be applied based on the business environment. In general, these issues will arise when: 1) the company is in start-up mode or is undergoing a major reorganization, resulting in frequent changes to sales territory assignments; 2) the sales force is targeting the low-end segments like SME and SOHO, which result in high volumes and high data volatility.

Higher-end segments on the other hand, eg corporate and global accounts, are well suited to remote usage because account volumes are low, account ownership is very stable, there are no marketing campaigns in the traditional sense of the term, and account updates are mainly attributed to the account manager himself. Daily synchronization is therefore not a critical requirement, and the volume of changed information between account manager and central database is low.

In conclusion, the advantage of using a CRM solution on the road in offline mode has to be balanced by the non-negligible usage constraints it imposes on the business, namely daily synchronization for users, the potential for inaccurate central reporting and the introduction of rigid, difficult-to-apply planning processes with resource requirements for both the business and IT.

The recommendation is that offline usage should be limited to sales reps who cannot do their jobs without it (eg working with a customer in front of a laptop, or call preparation and call reporting for multiple customers during the day). PDAs represent a valid offline alternative in some environments. Online usage should be maintained for the rest – who have to connect to the network in any case to check their e-mail. High-speed access like ISDN or ADSL should be provided to such users, and the architecture should be appropriately sized to be able to provide acceptable response times. If there is a pressure to get users working offline, then this should only be done in a subsequent phase, once the CRM project is stabilized in terms of processes and data procedures.

CHAPTER SUMMARY

▌ To limit project exposure to organizational change and company politics, break down your large-scale CRM vision into sufficiently small tactical initiatives with a life cycle that is well inside the half-life of the average executive's time in office.

▌ Once you've selected a CRM solution, you can't just sign a blank cheque to a systems integrator or a big-X consulting firm and expect them to do the job. You need an in-house centre of excellence that is in it for the long haul, so that crucial business knowledge and technical expertise can be retained in-house.

▌ As a customer-facing function, CRM requires an IT organization with a horizontal component that cuts across traditional boundaries and fiefdoms. This could lead IT to lean towards solutions that are biased more towards its internal organization than to the CRM business requirement.

▌ The waterfall method, with its rigidly contractual, life-cycle approach, can take over a year to produce meaningful results. It is clearly inappropriate for CRM, which is essentially a moving target. And moving targets are best handled as part of an iterative process, with three- to four-month cycles based on workshops and a prototype.

▌ The RFP-based approach, with its long-drawn-out package evaluation process based on an SoR, followed by the detailed customization of the chosen product, yields a final deliverable that is often unusable. Keep requirements short (no more than 30 pages) and focused on basic processes, and then let the vendors show you during a demonstration how they address those processes.

▌ The advantages of using a laptop on the road in offline mode has to be balanced by the non-negligible usage constraints it imposes on the business, namely daily synchronization for users, the potential for inaccurate central reporting, and the introduction of rigid, difficult-to-apply planning processes with resource requirements for both the business and IT.

Part IV

CRM risk analysis

12

Risk analysis

WHAT IS COVERED IN THIS RISK ANALYSIS?

The risk analysis in Table 12.1 is a checklist summary of the main elements of each chapter, summarized into question form. It has no pretension of being a complete risk analysis for CRM projects, because that would necessarily have to include elements common to all projects, not just CRM projects, which is beyond the scope of this book.

HOW TO USE THIS RISK ANALYSIS

This risk analysis is intended to be completed after having read the whole book – or alternatively after finishing each chapter. The answers to the questions are therefore based on the information provided in this book. Completing the questionnaire without reading the book first could lead to inaccurate answers, because of different meanings that could be attributed to certain terms. For example, the term 'pilot' can sometimes be a loosely defined term, which can mean either a trial implementation followed by a go/no-go decision for roll-out, or a phased roll-out with no option for backtracking. In this questionnaire, it is the former definition that is implied.

HOW TO INTERPRET THE RESULTS

As for the organizational readiness rating at the end of Chapter 3, the objective of this analysis is to make you think about your own situation overall, and not to pigeon-hole you into a given category based on mathematical precision. The final score categories are fairly broad, and how confident you feel about a particular issue is ultimately more important than your score for that issue.

A word of caution for those who would be tempted to use the results from a strictly mathematical point of view: regardless of the average score for a particular risk group, or even the total score, any risk factor of 3 could jeopardize the project and should therefore be individually addressed. Lastly, score 1 for questions that are not applicable to your project.

Table 12.1 *CRM risk analysis questionnaire*

Project Definition	
Organizational readiness rating (Chapter 3)	Score for organizational readiness rating: 1 = 15–21, or high organizational maturity; 2 = 8–14, or medium organizational maturity; 3 = less than 7, or low organizational maturity.
Business case and benefits (Chapter 4)	The business case and benefits are: 1 = readily understandable, and easily measurable; 2 = more or less understandable, but not easy to measure; 3 = difficult to understand, and difficult to measure.
Project scope (Chapter 6)	The project scope is: 1 = clearly reasonable, with limited objectives in one functional area; 2 = reasonable, but with multiple objectives in one functional area; 3 = clearly unreasonable, with multiple objectives in more than one functional area.
Cross-functional project team (Chapter 6)	Regardless of the project scope, the project team is: 1 = cross-functional, with agreement on long-term objectives from multiple functional areas, and with actual representation from those functional areas; 2 = cross-functional, with upfront agreement on long-term objectives from multiple functional areas, but with ongoing representation limited to a single functional area; 3 = comprised of members from a single functional area, with no agreement on long-term objectives from other functional areas, and no ongoing representation from other functional areas.

Table 12.1 *continued*

Project Definition

Executive sponsorship (Chapter 5)	The executive sponsor from the business is: 1 = identified, active and committed; 2 = identified, but passive; 3 = unknown, or the CEO, or it is an IT-led project.
Dedicated project owner working for executive sponsor (Chapter 5)	To ensure the day-to-day running of the project from the business side, the executive sponsor has: 1 = appointed a dedicated project owner with a full reporting line to the executive sponsor, with the project part of the project owner's key objectives; 2 = appointed a part-time project owner with a dotted reporting line to the executive sponsor, and with the project not necessarily part of the project owner's key objectives; 3 = not appointed anyone, and will assume this function as an additional responsibility.

Budget Definition

Approval of capital (capex) vs expense (opex) budgets (Chapter 7)	In your company, budgets for capital expenditure (capex) and operating expenses or SG&A (opex): 1 = are grouped at project level as part of a single approval process; 2 = follow independent approval processes, and may or may not be linked to each other at project level; 3 = follow independent approval processes, and are biased in favour of capex, with opex not usually attributed to a project.
Data migration (Chapter 7)	In the budget, resources for data migration are: 1 = well defined, with a realistic number of heads requested; 2 = identified, but insufficiently quantified; 3 = vague or non-existent.
Change management – training (Chapter 7)	In the budget, change management resources for training are: 1 = well defined, with a realistic number of heads requested; 2 = identified, but insufficiently quantified; 3 = vague or non-existent.
Change management – process change (Chapter 7)	In the budget, change management resources for process change are: 1 = well defined, with a realistic number of heads requested; 2 = identified, but insufficiently quantified; 3 = vague or non-existent.
Change management – data quality (Chapter 7)	In the budget, change management resources for data quality are: 1 = well defined, with a realistic number of heads requested; 2 = identified, but insufficiently quantified; 3 = vague or non-existent.

Table 12.1 *continued*

Budget Definition

IT data operations (Chapter 7)	In the budget, IT resources for data operations are: 1 = well defined, with a realistic number of heads requested; 2 = identified, but insufficiently quantified; 3 = vague or non-existent.
Separate pilot budget (Chapter 7)	The pilot budget: 1 = has been separately defined, and conditions the rest of the project budget; 2 = is part of the full project budget, and does not condition the rest of the project; 3 = does not exist as such, ie a successful pilot with a go/no-go checkpoint is not a milestone for this project.
Upfront CRM software licence deal (Chapter 7)	Upfront software licences: 1 = have been purchased only for the pilot; 2 = have been purchased for the pilot and for the subsequent roll-out for the current year; 3 = have been purchased for the full project, including licences needed over the next year.
Who defines the budget? (Chapter 7)	Your budget was/will be defined by: 1 = someone with prior experience in CRM, or at least SFA, plus input from vendors or consultants; 2 = someone new to CRM, but with input from vendors or consultants; 3 = someone new to CRM, and without input from vendors or consultants.
Final numbers in dollars per user per year (Chapter 7)	The final numbers of your budget measured in dollars per user per year are: 1 = more than $5,000; 2 = $3,000–$5,000; 3 = less than $3,000.

International CRM Projects

Justification for an international project (Chapter 8)	The justification for an international CRM project is based on: 1 = a cross-border service and customer base requiring transactional data sharing; 2 = a service that is not cross-border, but that would benefit from standardization across certain functions (eg order management and customer service); 3 = reasons unrelated to a cross-border service or customer base (eg reduced costs, international reporting, international synergy etc).
Previous company experience of international projects (Chapter 8)	Your company has: 1 = prior experience in at least two large-scale international projects; 2 = prior experience in only one large-scale international project; 3 = no prior experience in international projects of any nature.

Table 12.1 *continued*

International CRM Projects	
Country buy-in (Chapter 8)	Buy-in from the countries or subsidiaries: 1 = is a fundamental and explicit objective for the project, with a clearly defined process in place built around an international project team; 2 = is an implicit objective, with an informally defined process in place and not necessarily built around an international project team; 3 = is not an objective, or would be nice to have, but is clearly not part of the project plan.
Level of access to country data by HQ (Chapter 8)	Data from the countries (especially in an environment with operating companies with country MDs): 1 = will only be accessible to HQ with country 'permission', at agreed reporting intervals, eg via weekly 'push' reporting; 2 = will be accessible to HQ without country 'permission', but at agreed reporting intervals, eg via weekly 'pull' reporting; 3 = will be freely accessible to HQ without country 'permission', at any time, ie via on-demand 'pull' reporting.
Number of functional versions of the software (Chapter 8)	There will be: 1 = one standard functional version for all countries; 2 = one standard functional version for the majority of countries, plus an additional version for one group of countries, with only minor differences; 3 = two or more functional versions for multiple countries, with non-negligible functionality enhancements.
International architecture for day one (Chapter 8)	The international architecture for day one is: 1 = decentralized, single instance per country; 2 = regionalized, single instance per region; 3 = centralized, single instance worldwide.
International experience of project manager (Chapter 8)	The project manager: 1 = has project-managed one or more international projects in the past three years; 2 = has no experience of international project management, but can rely on one or more key people on the project team who have had such experience; 3 = has no experience of international project management, and neither do the other key people on the project team.
Language used for user training (Chapter 8)	User training: 1 = will be in the local language in those countries that require it, including training materials and documentation; 2 = will be in English for all countries, but training materials and documentation will be translated into the local language; 3 = will be in English for all countries, as will be training materials and documentation.

Table 12.1 *continued*

International CRM Projects

| Level one support in the countries (Chapter 8) | Level one support in the countries:
1 = will be decentralized and in the local language;
2 = will be centralized, with intelligent call routing to local-language agents;
3 = will be centralized and in English for all countries. |

Pilot Project

Existence of a pilot (Chapter 9)	The pilot approach is as follows: 1 = an operational pilot of sufficient duration is a fundamental and explicit part of the project, whose success conditions the rest of the project; 2 = an operational pilot is an implicit part of the project, but its result does not explicitly condition the rest of the project; 3 = a pilot is not part of the project plan, which is based on a roll-out with no prior validation of business objectives, and with little provision for correcting operational problems that might arise.
Scope of the pilot (Chapter 9)	The scope of the pilot is: 1 = limited enough to be able to be halted or suspended without being viewed as a failure that needs to be officially dealt with; 2 = large enough so that any halting or suspension for whatever reason might need to be officially dealt with, resulting in the possible break-up of the project team; 3 = so large that it cannot be halted or suspended without being viewed as a failure that needs to be officially dealt with, resulting in the break-up of the project team.
Integration to other systems (Chapter 9)	Integration to other systems: 1 = is not part of the pilot, with no interfaces of any kind planned; 2 = is part of the pilot, with semi-manual or batch interfaces to other systems; 3 = is part of the pilot, with automatic, real-time interfaces to other systems.
UAT as part of the pilot (Chapter 9)	Traditional user acceptance testing (UAT): 1 = is not part of the pilot, with acceptance limited to proof-of-concept at a high level; 2 = is part of the pilot, but is flexible as to the level of documented processes required; 3 = is an integral part of the pilot, with contractual acceptance based on detailed scripted processes.
Choice of pilot group, site or country (Chapter 9)	The pilot group, site or country will be chosen: 1 = so as to minimize the disruptive influence of external factors that have no intrinsic relation to the business objectives of the pilot; 2 = so as to minimize the disruptive influence of external factors, but there may be political or organizational criteria over which there is no control;

Table 12.1 *continued*

Pilot Project

	3 = based primarily on political or organizational criteria that are not necessarily compatible with the business objectives of the pilot.
International pilot (Chapter 9)	For international projects, the pilot: 1 = will be limited to one country only, with no other international input until after a successful pilot; 2 = will be limited to one country only, but with functional input from multiple countries; 3 = will be across multiple countries, with full international input.

Sales Manager Buy-In

Sales manager buy-in as part of the project plan (Chapter 10)	Buy-in by sales managers: 1 = is a fundamental and explicit part of the project, whose success conditions the rest of the project; 2 = is an implicit part of the project, but does not condition the rest of the project; 3 = is not part of the project plan, which is based on a roll-out with no validation, implicit or explicit, from this group of users.
Process for sales manager buy-in (Chapter 10)	The process to be used for sales manager buy-in is: 1 = a one-day offsite workshop, mandatory for all sales managers and the sales director, which combines a business benefits presentation with a hands-on discovery session of the pilot solution; 2 = a half-day meeting, mandatory for all sales managers and the sales director, which combines a business benefits presentation with a demonstration of the pilot solution; 3 = a one- or two-hour meeting, with attendance not mandatory, which reviews the business benefits, but without the visual support of a demonstration.
Sales manager's presence during sales rep training (Chapter 10)	The presence of the sales manager during the training of his or her team: 1 = is mandatory, and the session will be cancelled in his or her absence; 2 = is mandatory, but other business priorities could limit his or her attendance, and the session would not be cancelled; 3 = is viewed as necessary, but takes second place behind other business priorities.

Organizational Change and Company Politics

Ability of the project to survive organizational change and company politics (Chapter 11)	The probability of the project surviving organizational change and company politics is: 1 = high, because of the limited scope and/or the support of more than one person at executive level; 2 = medium, because the scope is possibly too large and/or there is not sufficient additional support at executive level;

Table 12.1 *continued*

Organizational Change and Company Politics

	3 = low, because of the large scope and/or because it is essentially a one-person show at executive level.

Balance of Permanent Staff vs Consultants

Degree of reliance on consultants and integrators (Chapter 11)	The balance of permanent staff to consultants and integrators is:
	1 = good, and adequate resources have been budgeted for both business analysts and developers to work alongside consultants and integrators, ensuring that project momentum can be maintained once the consultants and integrators have left;
	2 = reasonable, and resources have been budgeted for both business analysts and developers to work alongside consultants and integrators, but are probably insufficient to ensure project momentum is maintained once the consultants and integrators have left;
	3 = poor, and inadequate resources have been budgeted for both business analysts and developers to work alongside consultants and integrators, virtually guaranteeing that project momentum cannot be maintained once the consultants and integrators have left.

IT Resistance to Organizational Change

Reorganizing IT for CRM (Chapter 11)	The requirement for IT to reorganize to include a new horizontal CRM group, which cuts across the traditional vertical departments:
	1 = is fully recognized at IT executive level, and has been discussed at departmental level;
	2 = is more or less accepted at IT executive level, but has not yet been discussed at departmental level;
	3 = is not recognized at IT executive level, and has not even been brought up at departmental level.

Traditional vs Workshop Requirements Gathering

Identification of requirements (Chapter 11)	Business requirements have been/will be identified via:
	1 = combined workshop sessions with key users from cross-functional areas;
	2 = separate workshop sessions with key users from single functional areas;
	3 = one-to-one interviews between the analyst and key users.

CRM Product Evaluation Process

Method for evaluating CRM solutions (Chapter 11)	CRM product evaluations will be based on:
	1 = a requirements document of fewer than 40 pages, limited to processes and data for primary requirements;

Table 12.1 *continued*

CRM Product Evaluation Process

	2 = a requirements document of 40–100 pages, with processes and data for both primary and secondary requirements;
	3 = a detailed statement or requirements (SoR) of 100 pages or more, based on a traditional request for proposal (RFP) approach, and exhaustively itemizing all requirements (primary, secondary and nice to have).

Offline Usage with Synchronization

Offline usage with synchronization by the sales force (Chapter 11)	The sales force will use the CRM solution:
	1 = online, at the office or over the telephone network;
	2 = offline with synchronization, but in an environment with low data volumes and low data volatility;
	3 = offline with synchronization, and in an environment with high data volumes and high data volatility.

Risk Group	Risk Factor	Level (1 to 3)
Project definition	Organizational readiness rating	
	Business case and benefits	
	Project scope	
	Cross-functional project team	
	Executive sponsorship	
	Dedicated project owner working for executive sponsor	
Budget definition	Approval of capital (capex) vs expense (opex) budgets	
	Data migration	
	Change management – training	
	Change management – process change	
	Change management – data quality	
	IT data operations	
	Separate pilot budget	
	Upfront CRM software licence deal	
	Who defines the budget?	
	Final numbers in dollars per user per year	
International CRM projects	Justification for an international project	
	Previous company experience of international projects	
	Country buy-in	
	Level of access to country data by HQ	
	Number of functional versions of the software	
	International architecture for day one	
	International experience of project manager	
	Language used for user training	
	Level one support in the countries	
Pilot project	Existence of a pilot	
	Scope of the pilot	
	Integration to other systems	
	UAT as part of the pilot	
	Choice of pilot group, site or country	
	International pilot	
Sales manager buy-in	Sales manager buy-in as part of the project plan	
	Process for sales manager buy-in	
	Sales manager's presence during sales rep training	
Organizational change and company politics	Ability of the project to survive organizational change and company politics	
Balance of permanent staff vs consultants	Degree of reliance on consultants and integrators	
IT resistance to organizational change	Reorganizing IT for CRM	
Traditional vs workshop requirements gathering	Identification of requirements	
CRM product evaluation process	Method for evaluating CRM solutions	
Offline usage with synchronization	Offline usage with synchronization by the sales force	

Risk Total
40–66   Low risk
67–93   Moderate risk
94–120 High risk

Part V

Case studies

13

Case studies

CASE STUDY 1 – PHARMACEUTICALS (SUCCESSFUL PROJECT)

The company

The company is a European subsidiary of one of the top 10 pharmaceutical companies, with revenues of over US $500 million and a sales force of over 600 sales reps and sales managers. The year was 1995 and, in case you think that's a bit far back to be relevant today, the reverse is actually true, because at the time you didn't have the hype you have today (the term 'CRM' wasn't invented yet, and there weren't any CRM tools, period). Those companies that succeeded therefore did so by tackling the business problem first and then addressing the technical solutions afterwards. This case study therefore reads like a textbook example of how to launch and manage a CRM project.

The business problem

'Customer service' is not a term one would normally apply to the pharmaceutical industry, but it is nonetheless a very real requirement, since doctors can call up the pharmaceutical company that manufactures the drugs they prescribe. The main reasons would be for medical information about a product, eg a patient comes to a doctor to be jabbed with a new vaccine and the doctor realizes he forgot to put it in the fridge when he bought it the day before, and needs to know if it is still usable. Other reasons would be to request product samples, or to register for a company-sponsored event. Pharmaceutical companies usually put these customer interactions into two distinct categories: 'medical' and 'operations'.

Like most pharmaceutical companies, this one handled medical and operational questions separately, which had two major drawbacks. Firstly, it required the customer to deal with separate departments, usually not staffed to deal with enquiries; customers were therefore either put on hold or transferred – when they didn't simply hang up. Secondly, the absence of feedback between departments ensured that medical and operations often remained 'blind' on issues that might otherwise concern the other department. For example, an unusual recurrence of a question on product X could be the result of a medical issue, a promotional issue or even a competitor campaign – which should normally be channelled to marketing so that the appropriate corrective action could be taken. In reality, of course, this rarely happened because – to put it mildly – the left hand didn't know what the right hand was doing.

Even though most product-related questions were repetitive (a pharmaceutical product usually generates about 20–30 FAQs, what passed for customer service was characterized by unanswered questions, lost calls and an absence of feedback between medical and operations. There was also no standardization of medical information across functions, eg multiple versions of questions and answers (Q&As) existed for each department, each with its own 'official' answer (all of which were of course 'medically' correct, but nonetheless inconsistent).

The project context

On the operations side, the company had made enormous progress in the space of just two years in reorganizing its sales and marketing from separate, product-oriented organizations to a customer-centric organization. Today this would be called CRM; at the time it was simply called 'being customer-centric'. At the origin of this hugely successful transformation was a very basic business problem: one of the company's best-selling drugs, which contributed a significant chunk to annual sales, was being threatened by the arrival of generics. Simply put, the CEO had to find a way to stave off this potential disaster-in-the-making, and one of the answers turned out to be differentiation through superior customer service.

As part of this transformation to a customer focus, a customer-centric information system and a data warehouse had been running for over a year, capturing all sales and marketing interactions against a single doctor database. A new SFA system had also recently been implemented with success. The business and IT had a solid partnership with mutual credibility, and both had built up a store of knowledge and experience in CRM that boded well for the future.

The organization was therefore at a very high level of customer, process and system maturity, and the logical next step was to address the issue of customer service.

Project approach

The executive sponsor (the operations director) assigned a dedicated project owner from the business to tackle the issue of customer service. This person then set up a cross-functional project team from marketing, sales, medical, clinical safety, HR and IT.

Besides the representative, cross-functional nature of the team, one of its key strengths was the strong belief in CRM brought to the table by three members of the project team:

▌ the clinical safety director, whose forward-thinking views on CRM were instrumental in getting the medical department to break out of its traditional 'librarian' role and adopt a proactive, customer-facing role with a service culture;

▌ the project owner from marketing, newly arrived in the company from the mail-order business;

▌ the IT project manager, a CRM advocate from a non-pharmaceutical background who'd managed the customer-centric information system, the data warehouse and the SFA projects implemented over the past two years.

In an industry very much characterized by people in the medical and related professions moving from one pharmaceutical company to another, these non-traditional outsider views were critical in encouraging people to think 'outside the box'.

The team kicked off a feasibility study, which had three main parts:

I *External input.* Doctors were invited to a customer feedback meeting and asked to give their views concerning 'customer service'. Not surprisingly, they wanted to deal with as few people as possible in as short a time as possible. This was particularly important when they had a patient in front of them and they needed a quick answer. They also wanted to be able to use the same channel for other interactions like adverse effects reporting, seminar/event registration etc without having to call their sales rep. The key feedback from this session, and a subsequent survey, was the requirement for a one-stop-shop call centre.

I *Internal input.* Monthly tracking of calls to the telephone switchboard (via the PABX) revealed a lost call rate of 15 per cent. There was also a one-week, company-wide survey, during which every person potentially in touch with customers filled out a log of who called and for what purpose. The analysis showed that questions were asked by physicians (39 per cent), pharmacists (15 per cent) and sales reps (13 per cent). These figures confirmed that there was a real need for product information.

I *Benchmarking.* In an attempt to compare themselves with the industry, competitors and non-competitors alike, a number of standard questions were prepared and calls made by doctors on the project team to other pharmaceutical companies. The results were very poor, with just one out of the 10 companies called able to provide an acceptable level of service. The key feedback from this was that most other companies were equally bad, and that there was a window of opportunity for differentiation through superior customer service.

In an attempt to take medical information out of its 'librarian' status, and create competitive advantage through real customer service that closes the loop with operations, the following business objectives were defined:

I a one-stop-shop contact centre for all inbound customer contacts, whatever their nature (medical information, documentation, samples etc) and whatever the channel (phone, fax, mail), with a unique phone number to be published in the national medical dictionary of prescribable products, ie the doctors' 'bible';

▌ reflecting the horizontal, customer-facing nature of the contact centre, it was to be jointly run by both the medical and operations groups (an organizational revolution, for those who know the pharmaceutical industry);

▌ no lost calls;

▌ FAQs, which constitute 80 per cent of all product-related questions, to be handled by non-specialists at the first point of contact, adequately supported by a knowledge base containing the official, company-validated answers;

▌ a first-call resolution rate of 80 per cent, ie the percentage of all calls to be answered at level one, without transfer to level two;

▌ any level two transfers not resolved while on the line to be closed within three days;

▌ one hundred per cent customer satisfaction six months after launch.

The project team now kicked into high gear, adopting the tried and tested approach used for the previous CRM projects, ie a two-day off-site JAD workshop to define processes and data, which would be all the more challenging in that for the first time they would be defining new processes and not just formalizing changes to existing processes. One week later, they had a 30-page requirements document, which enabled them to evaluate technical solutions.

Product evaluation and chosen solution

As for the other CRM projects of the past two years, the company once again found itself from a strategic and systems perspective clearly ahead of its time. The very concept of 'customer service' for doctors in the pharmaceutical industry was a novelty in the mid-90s, so it was no surprise that there were no packages on the market.

There were of course customer-service packages with call-centre software, but the processes around which these packages were based did not fit well with the required pharmaceutical processes, for the following reasons:

▌ A customer service package usually requires upfront customer identification as a prerequisite for continuing the call. When doctors call up, however, they'll usually just mumble their name in passing and then launch straight into their question. Now if you really want to work up their ire – or get them to hang up and prescribe a competitor product – start by asking them for personal details that have nothing to do with their problem, usually with a patient sitting in front of them. It's like when you call up a cab company and say 'Hi, I'm currently at location X and would like a cab to go location Y', and they almost cut you off by saying, 'I first need your name', as if they can't ask you that afterwards.

▌ Once on the line, a doctor can ask more than one question, each of which needs to be uniquely identified and tracked for reporting purposes. Just about all customer service packages are based on enquiries or tickets that represent a single item.

▌ When dealing with a customer, the call-centre agent has to be able to view customer interactions across all channels. Most service packages, especially in the mid-90s, were not yet on the CRM curve whereby all interactions for a customer were stored, and not just tickets or enquiries.

▌ Integration to the company's customer-centric information system meant that any call-centre software had to be consistent with its data model, especially the many-to-many relationship between customers and institutions (also known as affiliations). This requirement is specific to the pharmaceutical industry, and is absent in customer service packages.

▌ The system had to have a knowledge base for FAQs.

Adapting a traditional, procedural and process-heavy customer service package, then possibly interfacing it to a knowledge base from a different vendor and then interfacing it all to the company's own systems was clearly not a cost-effective proposition. Today you might be able to buy something off the shelf close enough to be able to customize, but this was not even an option in 1995. So a decision was reached fairly quickly to build the required system.

The project team subsequently designed a solution to handle the following high-level processes:

▌ To address the FAQs, which would constitute over 80 per cent of all calls, the contact-centre agents would rely on a keyword-driven knowledge base, containing a list of official, company-validated questions and answers. Any question not part of the official FAQ list would be logged against the enquiry, and the call transferred to a doctor who would be able to view the same enquiry through basic workflow.

■ After successfully answering the enquiry, the agent would then ask the caller whether he or she wanted a follow-up validation fax or letter on an official company letterhead and signed by an authorized medical authority. This would trigger the printing of the appropriate page, which would then be signed and manually faxed or stuffed into an envelope (automation would come later and depend on actual volumes).

■ The agent would then ask for the caller's name and address, which it was hoped would be provided, to enable a check against the information in the central doctor database. This would enable continuous monitoring and improvement of data quality.

■ An enquiry would be fully owned by the level one agent, even if it went to level two. Any fax or mail follow-up, or any request for literature that required a walk to the nearby cabinet of product literature would always be handled by the owner of the enquiry, who would carry it out during slack time or any other time during the day. In order to guarantee the highest level of service and job motivation for the agents, excessive workflow and Taylorization were ruled out right from the start.

■ Full two-way integration with the customer-centric information system on a nightly basis would enable: 1) call-centre agents to be aware of any other prior customer interactions, eg sales calls or marketing interactions from other channels; 2) sales reps to be aware through their SFA laptops of any calls made by their customers to the contact centre that occurred the day before.

IT designed a screen prototype based on these processes (one week) and then worked with a software services company to produce a working prototype (two months), which was then given to two of the future call-centre agents for process validation (two weeks). The corresponding feedback resulted in refining the prototype to produce the finished product (four months), which was then system-tested (one month) in time for an on-schedule implementation.

The resulting solution had the following features:

■ a keyword-driven Q&A knowledge base populated with FAQs;

■ online access to customer addresses and contact history;

■ facilities for reply by phone, fax or mail;

▌ workflow routing of non-FAQs from level one non-specialists to level two specialists;

▌ e-mail routing of non-medical requests to relevant departments within the company (eg samples, event registration);

▌ e-mail routing to the clinical safety department of all drug adverse effects logged by the level one agents;

▌ an interface to the sales and marketing data warehouse, enabling enterprise-wide integration.

A pilot was not considered necessary to test the new system and processes for the following reasons:

▌ There was no external publicity made for the launch of the new department (this was to follow later), and therefore no customer expectations to meet.

▌ There were no potentially recalcitrant users to placate or changed processes to monitor. It was a newly created department, with highly motivated staff eager to start.

▌ The main requirement of the new department was to be able to answer FAQs over the phone. In the worst-case scenario, with the complete system down, call-centre agents could still meet this objective using a stand-alone version of the knowledge base on their PCs. No online customer identification and interfacing to the data warehouse would only impact internal reporting, not customer satisfaction.

Results

All of the business objectives were either met or exceeded. In the resulting two-tier organization, non-specialist customer service reps at the first point of contact ran at a 'first-call resolution rate' of around 90 per cent (as against the original target of 80 per cent), with the remaining 10 per cent transferred to specialists.

FAQs, which previously took up to a week or more to be answered (when they were answered at all), were now being handled in less than 30 seconds, with the full enquiry wrapped up in a minute. Customer satisfaction measured from an independent outside company was 99 per cent within the first month.

Most pharmaceutical companies would already consider it a remarkable achievement to be able to know how many questions were asked each month, regardless of which ones and for which products or therapeutic class, and by which doctors and pharmacists. Here we had a company that was able to operate down to the most detailed level, ie able to identify how many times a particular question was asked about a particular product in a particular therapeutic class – and by which doctor or pharmacist in the company-wide doctor database. There was even a screen called the 'Top Ten', which showed over any period of time (day, week, month) the top 10 questions asked.

Close-the-loop, weekly, cross-functional meetings were held between the contact centre and other departments to review the top questions asked and identify any trends that would require corrective action from a particular department to eliminate or reduce the occurrence of a particular question.

Time-scales

Total elapsed time was: 1) six months from project launch through feasibility study to formal definition of objectives; 2) nine months from definition of objectives through requirements, evaluation, development and implementation.

Three months later

The contact centre soon moved beyond just answering FAQs. It served as a means to monitor and improve data quality. Usually doctors in a hurry and used to poor service will hesitate to spend non-productive time providing their name and address details to a call-centre agent. However, with service now characterized by the phone being picked up in three rings or less, and FAQs answered within the space of 20 seconds (compared to days or weeks beforehand), callers were only too happy to show their gratitude by allowing the agent fully to check their name and address against the company's central database.

Probably the most business-sensitive use of the contact centre was the ease and speed with which the company was able to handle official communication about mad cow disease, which broke out in 1997. Whereas other companies had to scramble frantically to set up or outsource a dedicated phone number and call centre to handle queries, all that was needed was to define a number of FAQs reflecting the company's official line on the subject and put it in the knowledge base – in literally 48 hours.

One year later

There was a 50 per cent increase in the number of questions answered, with the first-call resolution rate still above 90 per cent, and customer satisfaction still at 99 per cent.

During a major product launch, the number of calls per day increased fivefold during the first few weeks after launch, providing vital feedback, which enabled quick corrective action, eg for product packaging and documentation. As new questions were also logged (ie those not yet in the knowledge base), multiple occurrences could be identified, and new FAQs could be set up on a weekly basis following product launch.

The only black spot on the horizon was a classic case of resistance to organizational change. This concerned the sales force, who did not initially adhere to the project, out of a fear that this channel could over time threaten their livelihood by replacing their face-to-face channel as the main source of information for doctors. Despite official communication to the contrary, there was an implicit boycott of this new channel by the sales force, to such an extent that a significant part of the sales force did not, as requested, publicize the service to their doctors during their visits! It took almost two years before the sales force came to accept that the one-stop-shop contact centre was simply one more component of the channel mix and in no way threatened the traditional face-to-face sales channel. By then, they themselves had become frequent callers to the contact centre, now convinced of the benefits of having access to the same up-to-date product information provided to their customers.

Two years later

I Creation of an official e-mail address, and opening up of a Web site as an official channel through which doctors could ask questions.

I Recognition of the department by a national institute of quality management.

I Quality of service now controlled by audit, in addition to customer satisfaction surveys.

Main lessons learnt (on the plus side)

As this was the third in a series of successful CRM-related projects, both the business and IT had already reached a level of experience whereby they were simply applying the best practice learnt over the years:

■ executive sponsorship, and a dedicated project owner from the business;

■ a clear business case with measurable objectives;

■ a cross-functional team with full business buy-in;

■ benchmarking;

■ customer input;

■ a workshop-based, iterative approach to systems deliverables.

Main lessons learnt (on the minus side)

The main lesson learnt on the minus side was about organizational resistance to change by the sales force. This was clearly foreseen right from the start, since it became apparent during the feasibility study. Despite all attempts to convince them that their jobs were not at stake, this reality was only accepted almost two years after launch.

Risk analysis questionnaire

The risk analysis questionnaire for the project is shown in Table 13.1. For those questions that are not applicable, the corresponding score is a 1 (ie low risk).

CASE STUDY 2 – TELECOMMUNICATIONS (FAILED PROJECT)

The company

The company is a start-up B-to-B European telco, selling voice and data to all market segments, from SMEs through to large corporate accounts.

Table 13.1 *CRM risk analysis questionnaire for Case study 1*

Risk Group	Risk Factor	Level (1 to 3)
Project definition	Organizational readiness rating	1
	Business case and benefits	1
	Project scope	2
	Cross-functional project team	1
	Executive sponsorship	1
	Dedicated project owner working for executive sponsor	1
Budget definition	Approval of capital (capex) vs expense (opex) budgets	1
	Data migration	1
	Change management – training	1
	Change management – process change	1
	Change management – data quality	1
	IT data operations	1
	Separate pilot budget	3
	Upfront CRM software licence deal	1
	Who defines the budget?	1
	Final numbers in dollars per user per year	1
International CRM projects	Justification for an international project	1
	Previous company experience of international projects	1
	Country buy-in	1
	Level of access to country data by HQ	1
	Number of functional versions of the software	1
	International architecture for day one	1
	International experience of project manager	1
	Language used for user training	1
	Level one support in the countries	1
Pilot project	Existence of a pilot	3
	Scope of the pilot	3
	Integration to other systems	3
	UAT as part of the pilot	3
	Choice of pilot group, site or country	3
	International pilot	1
Sales manager buy-in	Sales manager buy-in as part of the project plan	1
	Process for sales manager buy-in	1
	Sales manager's presence during sales rep training	1
Organizational change and company politics	Ability of the project to survive organizational change and company politics	1
Balance of permanent staff vs consultants	Degree of reliance on consultants and integrators	1
IT resistance to organizational change	Reorganizing IT for CRM	1
Traditional vs workshop requirements gathering	Identification of requirements	1
CRM product evaluation process	Method for evaluating CRM solutions	1
Offline usage with synchronization	Offline usage with synchronization by the sales force	1
Risk Total		**53**

40–66 Low risk
67–93 Moderate risk
94–120 High risk

The business problem

Surprising as this may sound, there was no business problem in the generally accepted sense of the term (eg improved forecasting, a shorter sales cycle, increased market share etc) for the simple reason that there was negligible business at the time the project was launched. How was this possible? Read on.

The project context

The year was 1997. Two years after the liberalization of telco B-to-B services in the major European countries, both national and foreign telcos were setting up shop at a frenetic pace, trying to chip away at the market share of the incumbent carriers (the PTTs), and to stake a claim in the new telco sector, which at that time promised to be an El Dorado.

The company was therefore in start-up mode, recruiting people at a massive rate, with numbers doubling every six months. The key decision makers for the new company weren't all in place yet, not even the CEO and the VP of sales. Both these key functions were being handled in the interim by other people. The IT department, however, already had its key players in place and drove the decision to launch an SFA project, the reasoning being that the sales force that would be recruited over the following nine months (which would number in the hundreds) would not be able to function correctly without an SFA system. In the absence of a VP of sales, there was no executive sponsorship outside of a limited role by the acting marketing director.

Product evaluation and chosen solution

A project team was set up with the limited people available at the time and, with the help of a big-X consulting company, started out with an initial requirements analysis based on interviews with a small number of people. This was followed by a product evaluation phase, which led to the selection of a big-league SFA vendor that had just set up shop in the country, with the telco as its first account.

Project approach

Insufficient internal resources

With no executive sponsor or full-time IT project manager, there was no choice but virtually to hand over the project to the consulting company.

The consulting company used the traditional waterfall approach and, since IT had no experience of the RAD/JAD prototyping approach normally associated with package implementations, they had no reason not to feel comfortable with this.

In the absence of any meaningful control and management by the client, all they had to show two months later was a thick requirements document, the result of interviewing a wide variety of people. Unhappy with what they perceived as unacceptable results, the company let go of this particular consulting firm and embarked upon what they considered a safer strategy. Instead of a single integrator responsible for the project from end to end, they took on two separate integrators: 1) one upstream for the design and configuration, responsible for delivering the version; 2) another downstream for system testing and implementation, responsible for actually putting the solution in place.

The new upstream integrator also adopted the traditional waterfall approach. Finally, given the company's inexperience in this type of project, change management was not identified and resourced, and was to be factored in much later as an IT responsibility.

A system designed by marketing for salespeople

Given the lack of people from sales to provide input, and general unavailability of people, who were more than overworked in their normal jobs that had nothing to do with the project, most of the requirements ended up coming from the marketing department. Not surprisingly, marketing's idea of a good SFA system was one with as much profiling information as possible, so that they could segment and target down to a fine level. Of course, the implicit assumptions were that they would be adequately staffed to provide and maintain all of this information, and that sales reps would also contribute to maintaining its quality.

Marketing takes ownership of customer information

Another key marketing requirement was data quality, a laudable objective. The relative absence of project input from sales resulted in marketing taking ownership for all account data. Aware of the requirement for sales reps to have accurate and timely account information corresponding to their portfolio and market segment, marketing created an internal group whose role would be to create new accounts for the sales force with all the required information validated (address, postcode, parent company etc). Sales reps would not be allowed to create any accounts themselves; they would have to provide the marketing department with the essential information of name, address and tax ID, and marketing would validate this information against the central database, with verification from external data providers if necessary, and then determine if the account was indeed eligible for the sales rep's market segment and territory. Then and only then would marketing make the account visible in the sales rep's portfolio. Though sound in theory, there were two practical problems: firstly, there was no one from sales to validate this process, which was imposed by marketing; and, secondly, marketing was not sufficiently staffed to provide such a service.

A one-size-fits-all solution for all market segments

Another major business difficulty was the near impossibility of designing a one-size-fits-all SFA system for sales reps selling radically different products (simple and complex) to radically different market segments (low-end SMEs to high-end corporate and international accounts) with very different sales cycles (short and appointment-driven at the low end, long and funnel-stage-driven at the high end). And what limited sales input did find its way into the design was more from the high-end segments, which resulted in the final design being skewed towards selling complex products to large, multi-site corporate accounts with long sales cycles measured in months.

Insufficient vendor presence and product expertise

On the technical side, things were made difficult by an unstable national-language version of the SFA product. The relative inexperience of the local subsidiary, newly set up in the country and only beginning to come to grips with the product, didn't help things either. Product technical experience was lacking at the integrator level too – neither the upstream nor the downstream integrator had any knowledge of the vendor's product, and had to be trained first before being able even to start working.

A new project manager takes some radical decisions

The combination of the above factors, ie no IT project manager from the client side to manage the integrators, product inexperience at both the vendor and the integrator level, lack of business input from sales, an over-reliance on business input from marketing, an unstable product and finally a very hazy idea of what the final deliverable was to look like and achieve, meant that the project inevitably slipped.

By the time a newly recruited IT project manager came on board, the project was already four months late. This project manager, with a track record in both SFA and CRM in his previous company, conducted an informal two-week audit of all the players (business, vendor, integrators), the project approach (traditional waterfall with no prototyping, no input from sales and no pilot) and status (no tangible deliverables in sight), and took some radical decisions:

▌ He let go of the downstream integrator, who had no experience in SFA concerning implementation, training, support and the logistics of managing hundreds of remote users. Within a week, he had assembled a new downstream team by hand-picking the required resources from small to mid-size consulting companies he had worked with in his previous company.

▌ He outsourced the support function by setting up a contract with an external help-desk vendor, to prepare for the inevitably high number of calls that would follow the critical first few weeks of implementation.

▌ He defined a new integration organization with buy-in from all the newly arrived consultants. This was done by putting them all in a room for a day and, with the help of post-it notes stuck all over the walls, running them through all the configuration and implementation processes associated with an SFA project. The group then defined who would head up each process, and the handover requirements to make it work. For the very first time since the project started, people were at last aware of what needed to be done to deliver results, how to go about it and their role in making it happen.

I He got some sales reps and sales managers to provide input on the most recent version in development. This prototyping approach, though fairly late in the game, identified for the first time the over-engineering of the proposed solution from a marketing standpoint. Some key redesign decisions were made to make the product more sales-friendly, mainly by introducing dedicated screens for marketing, which sales would not be obliged to 'wade' through in their day-to-day use of the system. However, this meant another development/test cycle to incorporate these changes, which delayed things further, even though it now meant working towards a design that had at least a minimum of sales input.

Most of the fundamentals are still absent

With a newly reorganized team, a rescoped project, clearly defined deliverables and an actual target date, there seemed to be at last a semblance of normality to the project (at least for those with no prior SFA project experience). However, most of the fundamental prerequisites were still absent, ie executive sponsorship from sales, clear business deliverables and across-the-board consensus from the sales groups for each market segment on processes and screen design.

The project manager also tried to incorporate other best-practice guidelines to increase the chances of a successful implementation, but this proved difficult to achieve:

I *An operational pilot.* Because the project was already four months late, such a phase was deemed not politically possible because, the reasoning went, it would push out the implementation date even further, and the business was waiting for results.

I *Change management.* Having user training defined and run by the business, to ensure it was process-oriented and yielded the key deliverable of 'a day in the life of a sales rep', was not possible, for the simple reason that change management was never built into the original project plan. Training was viewed as an IT responsibility. Drawing on his experience of previous SFA projects, the IT project manager therefore had to run around himself and locate some cooperative sales reps and sales managers and put together some real-world case studies to form the basis of the training.

I   *Sales manager buy-in.* Briefing and training sales managers on the system first, and getting their approval for the new processes were not possible because they didn't have the time. A two-hour briefing session was nonetheless arranged, which only half attended anyway, and which turned very quickly into a discussion about the pros and cons of such projects. The general consensus was that this was not the time to be implementing a system of this scope.

I   *Sales manager presence at training sessions.* Mandating the presence of sales managers at their team's training session, to anticipate objections, placate Luddites and ensure process buy-in, was agreed to in theory, but inevitably many could either not attend or only attend half a day, as their normal jobs took priority.

Results

When implementation finally occurred (three months after the arrival of the new project manager), it was still very clearly an IT-led affair. Even with some of the fundamentals now incorporated into the project plan, it was still touch and go. From a technical and logistics standpoint, the implementation went relatively smoothly: that is to say, it was characterized by the usual hassles, malfunctions, bugs, hardware breakdowns, data migration, miscommunication, training attendance, staff illness, support issues and general Murphy's law considerations associated with all SFA implementations, even successful ones. When all was said and done, they were simply making the best of a bad situation. The picture painted one month after implementation, confirmed by a user survey, was not a pretty one:

I   *Low usage.* Usage was dismally low, as measured by system access and synchronization logging. The reply to the question, 'How often do you use the system?' was 'frequently' 15 per cent, 'little' 50 per cent and 'not at all' 35 per cent, which equated to 85 per cent of the people effectively not using the system.

I   *Ineffective training.* Training was quite effective from a 'mechanical' point of view, but not in terms of the underlying processes. In reply to the question, 'How user-friendly do you consider the system?', 53 per cent of respondents replied that it was user-friendly and 13 per cent replied it was very user-friendly. However, it was generally ineffective in terms of buy-in to the underlying processes. A lot of sales reps, especially during sessions where their sales managers were absent, had no qualms about saying there was no way they would operate in such and such a manner. In some sessions, this 'defiance' was led by the sales managers themselves! The general comments were, 'Whoever dreamt up these processes don't know how we really work' and, 'We never validated any of this anyway'.

■ *No business leadership.* With no business sponsor, no change management resources and those users from marketing who helped design the system lacking the credibility to speak on behalf of sales, there was no one for either the users or IT to turn to for conflict resolution. So once again IT ended up trying to fill a business role for which it was not equipped: doing surveys, organizing meetings with users and jumping on trains visiting regional offices to spread the gospel.

■ *Incomplete data migration.* The promised migration of sales reps' prospecting data from their personal Excel and Access systems to the new SFA system never took place. They were expected to rely solely on centralized data provided from marketing. Not surprisingly, many continued to use the old systems that contained their personal data.

■ *Conflict over account ownership.* The centralization of account creation by marketing and the disabling of this feature for the sales reps met with much resistance. As far as most sales reps were concerned, sales owned the data, not marketing. And the inadequately staffed marketing department was unable to provide a quick turnaround time for new account creation for the sales force. So once again, many users continued to use their old systems.

■ *Synchronization issues.* The logistics and the procedural aspects of managing remote usage was a major factor in user dissatisfaction. There were two main reasons: 1) Most users synchronized once or twice a week, instead of daily as required; central reporting was therefore always inaccurate. 2) Because of the start-up nature of the company, account data were being updated almost daily as the result of marketing campaigns and account qualification by external call centres. The volatile data meant that synchronization times were unacceptably high, even for users connecting daily. Mass updates and new account imports from data providers were run over the weekends, which required users to synchronize specifically on a Friday, not work the weekend and expect high synchronization times on the Monday. Not surprisingly, this proved extremely difficult to plan in a sales environment. These hassles were even more difficult to swallow given that the majority of the sales force were office-based and not on the road. Their desktop PCs were locked during these synchronization sessions, which instead of lasting a few minutes could end up lasting 15–30 minutes or more, at which juncture the users would either cancel the operation, thereby ensuring further grief next time round, or simply get IT to reload their PCs completely with their account portfolio.

▌ *Poor data quality.* The previous two issues were the main contributors to poor data quality, which was probably the strongest incentive not to use the system. In reply to a question on data quality, only 30 per cent of users considered that they had data of a sufficient level of quality to enable them to work properly.

▌ *Parallel reporting via Excel.* Official sales reporting and forecasting continued to be provided from Excel spreadsheets put together before the project started. Sales managers therefore were still required to provide their reporting via Excel. There was no business requirement for official reporting to be provided by the new SFA system, and therefore little incentive to come to grips with it.

▌ *Information overload.* Even after descoping most of the initial requirements and hiding the marketing profiling information on separate screens, the general consensus was that even then there was still too much information. In reply to the question, 'How do you view the amount of information on your screens?', 47 per cent of respondents replied that it was 'too much'. Most users polled, especially those from the low-end SME segments, wanted just about everything stripped out except for name, address and basic profiling and activity information (ie the prospecting equivalent of name, rank and serial number). They were essentially asking for the SFA tool to be descoped to the equivalent of a contact manager.

■ *Organizational inertia.* Last but not least, the organization was in continuing flux: a new CEO came on board just before implementation; a major sales reorganization was on the cards two months after implementation; the long-awaited VP of sales was about to be hired three months after implementation. There was understandably, therefore, a general inertia and a wait-and-see attitude, which did not encourage the business to deal seriously with any of the above issues.

Three months later

This situation lasted for a few months, during which IT brought in once again a new consulting company to manage the project, and the IT project manager who had run the implementation now reported to the consultants. The main thrust of this new consulting company was to get official requirements documented, generating another series of meetings with the business. By the time the VP of sales was at last on board, the status of the project was more or less unchanged, with the business still not in the driver's seat and system usage still well below 50 per cent. Three months after implementation, by the time this chronicle ends, a major new version of the software was planned, whose main feature was an even further simplification of the screens. But even this was put on hold pending a major account redistribution, which was to include complex cross-segment movements with a big impact on sales processes, and which effectively put a halt to rolling out any new version.

Time-scales

The total elapsed time from project launch through to the start of implementation was eight months.

Main lessons learnt (on the plus side)

The prototyping feedback from sales that followed the project reorganization and rescoping after the arrival of a full-time IT project manager was essential in validating real, as opposed to perceived, requirements. While far from ensuring buy-in, it at least resulted in a first version that was a workable starting point for any future iterative work. If there had been a pilot phase, then this would no doubt have been an acceptable pilot version, ie subject to operational feedback and refinement.

Main lessons learnt (on the minus side)

On the minus side, the main lessons learnt read like a checklist of virtually all of the critical success factors and risk factors in this book. This project actually managed to combine them all:

▌ no business case;

▌ no executive sponsorship;

▌ an IT-led project;

▌ a start-up environment with unstable processes;

▌ an insufficient budget;

▌ no change management resources;

▌ no sales rep buy-in;

▌ no sales manager buy-in;

▌ signing a blank cheque to a systems integrator;

▌ too many consultants, too few permanent staff;

▌ no pilot;

▌ poor data quality;

▌ using a traditional waterfall approach;

▌ the complexities of offline usage with synchronization;

▌ a vendor that had just set up shop in a country and had an unstable product and insufficient in-country expertise.

Now you would be justified in thinking that this company had a really bad IT department. However, there is an explanation for their blind insistence on implementing the system. The company was a start-up telco, and IT had a mandate to ensure that six to nine months down the line all basic systems were in place for the rapidly growing company to be able to function properly. After all, they also put a customer service system in place, and you could argue you don't need to wait for an official business case from an executive in customer service to know that you're going to need a customer service system. Ditto for billing. True, but sales is different, and this fact can only be understood by IT project managers who have managed SFA projects before and therefore understand the realities of sales and marketing. Unfortunately, there was no one at the time in IT who had any experience of SFA, so they understandably used the same line of reasoning they used for customer service and billing, ie viewing it as a prerequisite for the sales force to be able to function at all. It was inconceivable at the time for IT to ask themselves if the sales force really needed an SFA system – to them it would have been equivalent to asking if they needed a billing system. And, needless to say, neither the consultants nor the SFA vendors were going to suggest that now was not the time for a system of such scope.

With hindsight, the prudent option would have been just to leave them to muddle through with Excel, Access, Filemaker Pro or whatever. The boldest attempt at a system should have stopped at a contact manager, with the sole objective of standardizing the data format to facilitate data migration at a later stage to an SFA product. The main prerequisite for a sales force to function is a good prospecting list and a telephone, period. Sales reps see to the rest with their personality, product knowledge and selling skills. Nowhere does an SFA tool come into the picture – yet. Of course, the sales manager might not have much visibility on the progress of the team's pipeline, and there might be a lot of non-value-added work, and poor targeting and prospecting, but as long as orders come through and quotas are filled it can be said that the sales function is 'working'.

It also proved very difficult to design a one-size-fits-all SFA system for sales reps selling radically different products (simple and complex) to radically different market segments (low-end SMEs to high-end corporate and international accounts). The sales cycles are very different: short and appointment-driven at the low-end, long and funnel-stage-driven at the high end. Since you can't please all the people all the time, you end up pleasing only some of the people some of the time, which is not a solution. This question is further explored in Case study 3, where a satisfactory solution was found.

Finally, having separate systems integrators for upstream (requirements, design and configuration) and downstream (testing, implementation and support) is a recipe for disaster and finger pointing. Instead of one end-to-end integrator seeing the big picture and having a vested interest in sorting out the inevitable difficulties along the way, two integrators are not incentivized to make it work, and will instead document themselves to death to ensure that they are 'clean' at the handover point – and in the meantime the client is wondering why things are not moving forward.

Risk analysis questionnaire

The risk analysis questionnaire for the project is shown in Table 13.2. For those questions that are not applicable, the corresponding score is a 1 (ie low risk).

CASE STUDY 3 – TELECOMMUNICATIONS: INTERNATIONAL PROJECT (SUCCESSFUL PROJECT)

The company

The company is a major B-to-B international telco, selling voice and data to all market segments, from SMEs through to large corporate and wholesale accounts. Though a major player in its home country, the company was essentially in start-up mode internationally, with new offices in Europe and Asia Pacific opening every few months in the period 1998–99.

The business problem

The fundamental objective of this project was CRM, though the term used at the time was 'customer care'. During its first few years of operation in the main European countries, the company focused on voice and data services to large corporate accounts, and the international subsidiaries of multinationals (mainly banks and insurance companies). As in most start-up environments, staff numbers were kept low until the business reached a critical mass. The organization was therefore more horizontal than vertical, ie people worked in cross-functional roles that required access to information outside their particular area of expertise. For example, in order to manage the customer relationship better and be aware of evolving customer requirements that could lead to additional sales, an account manager was also expected to have access to

Table 13.2 *CRM risk analysis questionnaire for Case study 2*

Risk Group	Risk Factor	Level (1 to 3)
Project definition	Organizational readiness rating	3
	Business case and benefits	3
	Project scope	1
	Cross-functional project team	3
	Executive sponsorship	3
	Dedicated project owner working for executive sponsor	3
Budget definition	Approval of capital (capex) vs expense (opex) budgets	2
	Data migration	3
	Change management – training	3
	Change management – process change	3
	Change management – data quality	3
	IT data operations	3
	Separate pilot budget	3
	Upfront CRM software licence deal	3
	Who defines the budget?	3
	Final numbers in dollars per user per year	1
International CRM projects	Justification for an international project	1
	Previous company experience of international projects	1
	Country buy-in	1
	Level of access to country data by HQ	1
	Number of functional versions of the software	1
	International architecture for day one	1
	International experience of project manager	1
	Language used for user training	1
	Level one support in the countries	1
Pilot project	Existence of a pilot	3
	Scope of the pilot	3
	Integration to other systems	3
	UAT as part of the pilot	3
	Choice of pilot group, site or country	3
	International pilot	1
Sales manager buy-in	Sales manager buy-in as part of the project plan	3
	Process for sales manager buy-in	3
	Sales manager's presence during sales rep training	3
Organizational change and company politics	Ability of the project to survive organizational change and company politics	3
Balance of permanent staff vs consultants	Degree of reliance on consultants and integrators	3
IT resistance to organizational change	Reorganizing IT for CRM	3
Traditional vs workshop requirements gathering	Identification of requirements	3
CRM product evaluation process	Method for evaluating CRM solutions	3
Offline usage with synchronization	Offline usage with synchronization by the sales force	3
Risk Total		**95**

40–66 Low risk
67–93 Moderate risk
94–120 High risk

billing and service information. Similarly, a network consultant, who was the customer's main point of contact after a sale, also required access to both sales and service information. Since customers usually purchased multiple services over time, the network consultant needed to manage the customer on a consolidated rather than on a contract-by-contract basis.

An enterprise-wide view of the customer, spanning both sales and service, was therefore the main business objective. Realistically, it was also accepted as a long-term goal, because there were three other immediate business problems to solve:

▌ The main one was improved revenue and network capacity forecasting in an explosive high-growth environment, with the established countries doubling every year and new countries opening up every few months. In such an environment, with all heads focused on revenue growth and no standard sales system in place yet, both local and consolidated reporting was done in Excel. This situation was rapidly reaching its limit, with sales and capacity forecasting becoming less accurate, less timely and more resource-intensive (impacting company financial reporting and network planning).

▌ The sales force was spending too much time on administration and reporting. Account managers were using a combination of Excel, Access and Exchange to manage their accounts, opportunities and activities. They then had to re-enter their updated opportunity pipeline into the standard Excel templates used for weekly forecasting. Needless to say, all this was eating significantly into prospecting and selling time.

▌ The sales force was also spending a lot of time exchanging e-mails back and forth with the other key players in the sales cycle (network consultants and bid management) about opportunity details and customer history. This information was needed by the other players to assist the account manager in driving an opportunity to the proposal stage. This inability to share information was not only an administrative burden, but it also increased the length of the sales cycle.

The project context

The project sponsor was the sales integration director, responsible for international sales. He recruited an international sales operations director to be the dedicated project owner for the day-to-day running of the project in conjunction with IT.

On the IT side, the director of corporate systems, a very knowledgeable and visionary person in terms of CRM, was able to build a working relationship with the key business executives in both sales and service. He also recruited a full-time person, an IT programme manager with a track record in both SFA and CRM, to work hand in hand with the project owner from the business. Besides managing the project and being the interface between the business and the package vendor, the IT programme manager also had the responsibility of setting up a centre of excellence based on the chosen CRM solution. Because of the rapidly changing, high-growth environment and the high costs proposed by integrators, IT placed an emphasis on permanent staff rather than on external consultants, thus ensuring that the knowledge stayed in-house.

The timeline set for the project was for all 13 countries (nine in Europe and four in Asia Pacific) to be operational within 12 months.

Product evaluation and chosen solution

A package had already been selected a year earlier following a detailed evaluation of five vendors, but the project was put on hold when the company merged with another telco six months later. The project was then revived in early 1998, the time at which this chronicle starts.

Project approach

A phased approach, starting with SFA

Though CRM was the ultimate destination, it was clear that the first component and piece of the puzzle was SFA. The project was therefore billed as such, ie an SFA project, not a CRM project. However, all project communication stressed this phased approach, making it clear that the ultimate objective was full customer care. This was essential in getting the cooperation of other functional areas right from kick-off, and not just of sales.

Managing the international factor

Even with active executive sponsorship, clear business objectives, a dedicated business owner and a full-time IT programme manager, there was still the international factor to be dealt with, ie managing the political and cultural aspects of an HQ-driven project in such a way as to obtain country buy-in and not rejection of yet another well-meaning corporate initiative. Each country had its own managing director, with a sales director in charge of sales for all market segments in that country, reporting via dotted line to the executive sponsor. In such an environment, a sales director in a country was first and foremost responsible to that country's MD, and if push came to shove the country organization would always take precedence over a dotted-line relationship to HQ.

This organizational reality was clearly a major concern for the programme manager, who in previous lives had seen international projects fail for this very reason. The business sponsor, owner and programme manager therefore agreed to place top priority on obtaining buy-in from each country, and only to wield the big stick as a last resort. In practice, this meant first getting a pilot working in one country, followed by buy-in from other countries at executive level, and finally getting buy-in at user level – all prior to implementation. The key principle at every stage of the way – communicated as such by the sponsors and the programme manager – was that the solution would not be imposed and that, if any country had critical requirements that were not met, then the team would go back and fix things. The bottom line was that, when the implementation team arrived in a country, it was to be with buy-in and by invitation, to ensure the in-country cooperation without which the project would not succeed.

Obtaining a budget for the pilot

Funding was first obtained for the pilot phase – and quite easily given the relatively small sums involved (for 30 people only – see the next section). Full funding for the rest of the project, however, would be dependent on a successful pilot.

Defining the pilot

There was then the question of whether to get input from all countries or to keep the pilot focused on one country only and then throw it open to the rest. The second option was taken, because of the number of countries (13) and the fact that it was a start-up environment with each country at a different maturity level. A country was therefore chosen for the pilot that had a suitable level of process maturity, and no regional offices to compound data problems and bandwidth issues.

Once a pilot country was chosen, a cross-functional team was set up within that country, with membership from the key players in the sales process:

▌ sales (the sales director, a sales manager and an account manager);

▌ marketing (the marketing director and the campaign manager);

▌ a network consultant (equivalent to tech sales in other industries);

▌ a bid manager (from bid support, the group that provides internal support to the account manager for complex bids);

▌ the IT programme manager;

▌ a consultant from the package vendor.

The objective of the pilot was proof-of-concept for a solution to the three short-term business problems outlined above, ie improved sales and capacity forecasting, reduced administration time for the account manager and information sharing with other players in the sales cycle.

A two-day JAD workshop was held, which focused on two main areas: 1) the information they wanted to see held against prospects and customers; 2) the reports they wanted to get out of the system.

This was summarized into a 10-page document, which served as the input for a prototype. The pilot was to be kept as simple as possible, with minimal deviation from the standard vanilla product. Subsequent-version evolution was to be driven by actual usage rather than documented requirements. It was therefore made very clear to the project team that the pilot was but a first version for proof-of-concept, and that richer features and all the wish lists that came out of the workshop would necessarily have to come later.

In order to simplify the project as far as possible, it was decided to build a standard application in English with dollar-based reporting (ie no local currencies, no local languages). As it was an international business selling standard products with monthly revenues reported in dollars, this was an acceptable solution.

The prototype was completed two months later, and demonstrated to the project team for validation. Unfortunately, not all of the sales managers could be present at this key session. Even the sales director's attention began to wane as the launch date neared and, though he still wholeheartedly supported the project, he made it clear that the company had some very important deals to close for the quarter, and he'd do his best but couldn't guarantee everyone's presence. At the end of the session, he simply said, 'It's great; just put it in place. This is important, so we'll deal with any issues as they arise'. This session demonstrated more then ever the difficulty of sustained commitment in a start-up environment with resource and time constraints.

In order to keep the pilot focused on the population who would make or break the project, the first version was rolled out only to the sales force; marketing and the other players in the sales cycle would come later.

Infrastructure-wise, as there were only around 30 users the pilot was implemented on a small NT server with users working online from the LAN. Though the solution did offer remote usage with synchronization, this feature was not even considered for the pilot phase because of the organizational and technical constraints associated with this mode of working, which have nothing to do with proof-of-concept.

Finally, though the training for the pilot would ultimately be the baseline for all countries, both the materials and training were done in the local language, to ensure maximum buy-in from the users.

Results

Stabilizing the pilot

Despite intense handholding and the implementation team being on the ground in the pilot country and speaking the same language, the first month of usage was just average, for the following reasons:

▌ Though the users were satisfied with the functionality and amount of information on the screens, they soon found out that the product was poor in terms of user-friendliness, with tabs all over the place and lots of buttons on each tab, and the obligation to press the save button on each tab before clicking on another tab. So if an account comprised four tabs, and users entered or changed information on each tab, they'd have to press a save button four times instead of just once. Inevitably, users complained of information not captured that they were sure they'd entered.

■ The combination of the latest version of the package and the latest version of the relational database system led to serious instability during a period of two weeks, with a complete database restore required on at least two occasions.

■ There were the inevitable bugs that made life difficult, but most were corrected very quickly (within the first month).

■ Sales manager buy-in was problematic. Because only half of them managed to attend the initial demo session prior to launch, some of them were only half-heartedly supporting the effort.

It took over two months for the above operational issues to be either ironed out or grudgingly accepted before there was a critical mass in terms of usage to enable the weekly reporting to be produced by the new system. When this first business objective was finally achieved, the sales force no longer had to do double entry into Excel, thereby freeing up at least half a day per week. The two sales support assistants were now able to complete the weekly forecasting in just two hours as opposed to the two days needed previously, leaving them free to concentrate on real sales support.

Validating the pilot internationally

The pilot then had to be validated internationally – a green light from one country does not mean you have international buy-in. A one-day international validation workshop was therefore held in a European capital, attended by a cross-section of sales directors, sales managers and account managers from all countries. The session started with the business sponsor reviewing the business objectives of the project, and stressing the crucial need for their buy-in in order to proceed. This was followed by a detailed demo of the pilot version, which was then followed by a series of breakout sessions focusing on subjects like customer profiling, information sharing by all players in the sales cycle, and integration to downstream order management and billing systems. At the end of the day came the critical moment, when a show of hands was required by each country to approve proceeding with the project and the pilot in its current form. If approval was not given, people would be asked what was needed to get them to a yes vote. Apart from some qualifiers as to the future direction of the project (appetites had been whetted when they saw the future possibilities), the verdict was a unanimous yes. So, four months after kick-off, there was an organizational green light from all concerned to roll out the pilot version across all 13 countries. Needless to say, the business case for the rest of the project was a formality, and approval came through very quickly.

With country buy-in obtained at senior management level, the next step was obtaining buy-in at actual user level. After all, just because a country's sales director says, 'Let's do it' doesn't necessarily mean the troops agree. So the project owner and IT programme manager did a 13-country road show over a period of two months, with a full day in each country.

The morning was devoted to a business presentation by the project owner, followed by a detailed demo of the prototype by the programme manager. The audience consisted of the MD, sales and marketing directors, and carefully selected key users from sales, marketing, network consulting and bid management. The emphasis was on buy-in, with the key message being that the solution would not be imposed and that, if any country had critical requirements that were currently missing, the team would go back and include them before implementation. Countries were also reassured that they would have full control over their data environment, ie corporate HQ would not have free, roaming access into country data, eg they would only be able to see sales forecasting that had been previously authorized by the country sales directors.

In the afternoon, the IT programme manager met key users one-to-one or in small groups to get a feel for the data situation (how many sources, what level of quality, what to migrate over, what to discard etc) and other potential issues that didn't surface during the meeting and that could impact the implementation later on. These sessions were critical in identifying sensitive issues that usually don't surface during a meeting with all the bosses present (eg broken-down processes, official procedures routinely ignored because of this, that or the other, behind-the-scenes scepticism because of a similar project initiative two years ago that bombed, etc). In most Asia Pacific countries, this is where you get to learn about the issues, because the deference to authority in Eastern cultures makes it virtually impossible to get any negative feedback in a meeting with one's bosses present – even when explicitly requested!

Building a centre of excellence

During this time the IT programme manager also started building up a centre of excellence in a European capital, recruiting people to head up departments in charge of requirements, training, configuration, data and implementation. When recruiting wasn't possible, the company turned to consultants. However, it proved impossible to fill the gaps with consultants from the big-X consulting firms with experience in SFA, as their approach was to be responsible for the whole project, rather than place their people in a 'body shop' environment run by the client. The company therefore turned to smaller outfits, which were only too glad to place consultants in such a large-scale international project, even though it was fully run by the client.

The vendor is acquired

One month later, an event of major proportions effectively put a halt to all progress – the package vendor was acquired by a competitor, and it took two months for a clear statement of direction to come out of the new entity in terms of which lines of products would be supported, halted and merged. It became clear that the product used for the pilot was no longer in the race, and the company took the decision to change horses in mid-stream.

But there was no in-house expertise on the new SFA product, and the implementation deadline based on the old SFA product was now a month overdue! The big-X consulting firms with significant experience on the new product were still not willing to join on anything less than a full end-to-end basis (at a substantial cost, which in any case wasn't budgeted). So the programme manager worked directly with the new vendor, who pulled out all the stops to ensure a fast transition to the new product: they located two configurators from two small consulting firms, and even put at their disposal a small development machine. For a period of one month, the requirements manager for the project worked with these two configurators in redesigning and reconfiguring a new product, based on the pilot version of the old product. Three months after the decision to switch products, a new pilot version was ready for implementation.

International implementation

Over the next eight months, this new version was implemented across 13 countries in Europe and Asia Pacific (suitably patched and enhanced along the way, because the rescue version was quite buggy, and did not adhere very well to vendor configuration guidelines).

One of the biggest challenges for this implementation was to provide local-language training as far as possible. This was a necessity for countries like France, Spain, Italy and Germany, while other countries were able to get by with training in English, eg the Nordic countries and the Netherlands. Local-language training involved identifying local training partners, training their trainers and gradually outsourcing this function, while all the time maintaining the quality of the training programmes by the central training group.

In a class of 13, everyone can't be top performers: there were therefore countries that were leaders and others that were followers. The leaders were those countries that understood the process benefits from the new system and the importance of data quality, and subsequently found the required business resources to make it work. Followers on the other hand were those that saw the system more as a reporting tool for HQ and saw support as an IT responsibility; the absence of sufficient business resources in these countries to drive process change and ensure data quality resulted in insufficient usage and consequently limited buy-in.

Data quality, not surprisingly, proved the biggest inhibitor to use. This was the norm in the follower countries, where the lack of change management resources in the business meant that data quality simply deteriorated to the point of unusability, at which stage they'd start the whole process over again, ie reloading a supposedly clean data set and retraining users. One country went through this cycle three times in 18 months.

IT and the business set up a change management organization during implementation, which got off to a difficult start characterized by some countries unable or unwilling to field the required resources from the business (see above). But this eventually matured to an international organization that coordinated both central and in-country requirements, resulting in a consensus for the features for each new version. Countries shared best practice during monthly meetings and quarterly workshops.

Time-scales

▌ Three months from kick-off to pilot implementation.

▌ Three months to stabilize the pilot.

▌ Nine months for implementation across 13 countries.

One year later

One year after the start of implementation, the environment had changed significantly, reflecting a rapidly changing business environment (remember that 1998/99 saw astounding growth in the telco sector):

▐ The high-end global accounts segment was spun off into a separate, international line of business.

▐ A new segment, SMEs, was created to address the high-volume low end of the market.

▐ Segmentation occurred, ie the in-country sales and marketing organizations, originally under single sales and marketing directors, now split off into separately managed segments, each with their own sales and marketing directors.

▐ The number of users had doubled, as had the size of the IT team, which had now become the centre of excellence for the product for the international organization.

▐ Marketing was brought on stream as well, allowing sales and marketing to share information for the first time.

▐ Confronted with the inescapable conclusion that dedicated business resources were needed to drive process change and ensure data quality, more and more countries began to take this seriously, creating new posts and staffing them with the right people.

New versions of the software came out every four months incorporating new features to address the needs of the changing organization, mainly enhanced profiling and opportunity management, and telemarketing and lead generation for the new SME segment. It was still a one-size-fits-all product for all segments, but increasingly each segment began to have its own specific requirements and timelines for deliverables, and it became clear that sooner or later the product would evolve into separate versions for each segment.

Two years later

The environment continued to change significantly, and the product along with it:

▮ The organization evolved beyond segmentation, with each segment now spun off into fully autonomous lines of business.

▮ The number of users had once again doubled, and the product was installed in five more countries (for a total of 1,500 users in 18 countries).

▮ The one-size-fits-all product for all segments had, not surprisingly, evolved into separate versions for each segment (but still part of a shared repository and development environment).

▮ There were two-way interfaces to/from a marketing database (for campaigning), external address providers (for address cleaning) and external call centres (for lead generation). For some lines of products, there were also interfaces to billing systems and the in-country PTT or incumbent carrier.

▮ Many other players in the sales cycle were brought on stream as well, realizing the third of the business objectives, which was to shorten the sales cycle. Players besides sales and marketing now included telesales, telemarketing, commercial contracts, dealer management, bid management and access management (the group that manages projects to bring new buildings, and hence new business, on to the network). Additionally, for some lines of products, there were also order management and customer service.

From a cost perspective (software licence costs excluded), all of this was achieved at significantly less than the costs of an integrator. With a permanent staff/consultant ratio of 3:2, an internal staff turnover of less than 10 per cent per year, and the low rates of the small consultancies willing to do the staff augmentation the big X shunned, the total annual cost per user of the home-grown centre of excellence was less than US $5,000. The equivalent cost for a partnership with an integrator would have been at least twice that – especially since the centre of excellence was based in a continental European country with much lower salary and consultancy rates than for the UK, which is the country on which the integrators based the pricing in their proposals. The cost factor notwithstanding, what was more important was that, with all the knowledge and key players in-house, the team was able to stay apace with the rapidly changing business environment described.

Finally, though the short- to medium-term business objectives were long since achieved, the ultimate CRM objective of an enterprise-wide view of the customer remained elusive. The main reason was the lack of both business sponsorship and IT awareness of CRM one year into the project. The original sponsor from the business was spun off into another organization, with a completely different system. On the IT side, the original IT director who helped launch the project moved into another function. In both cases, there resulted a vacuum, which three years after project kick-off had still not been filled.

Main lessons learnt (on the plus side)

The main lessons learnt on the plus side read like a checklist of most of the critical success factors and risk factors in this book:

▌ a valid business case;

▌ active executive sponsorship;

▌ a business-led project;

▌ a realistic project scope;

▌ an iterative, prototyping approach;

▌ an operational pilot;

▌ proper international project management;

▌ no over-reliance on consultants;

▌ no offline usage with synchronization.

Probably the most important of these was the proper management of the project from an international aspect: given the start-up nature of the company, any approach other than one based on country buy-in would have been doomed to failure before even jumping on to a plane.

Main lessons learnt (on the minus side)

On the minus side, we can also see some of the critical success factors and risk factors in this book:

▌ *Not enough change management resources in some countries.* This was not the result of any oversight, since the issues were clearly laid on the table right from project launch. It was more a question of a rapidly growing start-up environment in which resources could not always be committed to financially when requested. Therefore things sometimes had to be taken on faith. Those countries that suffered the most during this project were those with chronic data quality issues, which were only resolved once they saw they had no choice but to find and pay for these resources to make it work. The major mistake here was clearly on the HQ side, as it did not budget for these resources in the countries, thereby effectively passing them the buck.

▌ *Insufficient formalization of before/after metrics to demonstrate ROI.* Though the project yielded clear and undisputable ROI many times over, and this was recognized by the business users, there were no official pre-launch baseline metrics against which to measure these post-implementation benefits once the executive sponsor moved on. Though annual project funding was always obtained, it had to follow the same approvals process as for other projects. This was probably the biggest mistake made by the project team, which it paid for each subsequent year when budget time came around.

▌ *No dedicated buy-in from sales managers.* The start-up nature of the company and people's limited time made this objective unrealistic to expect.

▌ *Organizational change and company politics.* Both the business and the IT visionaries who initiated the project found themselves less than one year later in the wake of an international reorganization that effectively removed them from the picture. Though the project and solution were institutionalized over a period of three years – which was a measure of success – this was never really attributed to either person.

Risk analysis questionnaire

The risk analysis questionnaire for the project is shown in Table 13.3. For those questions that are not applicable, the corresponding score is a 1 (ie low risk).

Table 13.3 *CRM risk analysis questionnaire for Case study 3*

Risk Group	Risk Factor	Level (1 to 3)
Project definition	Organizational readiness rating	3
	Business case and benefits	2
	Project scope	1
	Cross-functional project team	2
	Executive sponsorship	1
	Dedicated project owner working for executive sponsor	1
Budget definition	Approval of capital (capex) vs expense (opex) budgets	3
	Data migration	1
	Change management – training	2
	Change management – process change	2
	Change management – data quality	2
	IT data operations	1
	Separate pilot budget	1
	Upfront CRM software licence deal	1
	Who defines the budget?	1
	Final numbers in dollars per user per year	1
International CRM projects	Justification for an international project	1
	Previous company experience of international projects	1
	Country buy-in	1
	Level of access to country data by HQ	1
	Number of functional versions of the software	1
	International architecture for day one	1
	International experience of project manager	1
	Language used for user training	1
	Level one support in the countries	1
Pilot project	Existence of a pilot	1
	Scope of the pilot	1
	Integration to other systems	1
	UAT as part of the pilot	1
	Choice of pilot group, site or country	1
	International pilot	1
Sales manager buy-in	Sales manager buy-in as part of the project plan	2
	Process for sales manager buy-in	2
	Sales manager's presence during sales rep training	2
Organizational change and company politics	Ability of the project to survive organizational change and company politics	1
Balance of permanent staff vs consultants	Degree of reliance on consultants and integrators	1
IT resistance to organizational change	Reorganizing IT for CRM	3
Traditional vs workshop requirements gathering	Identification of requirements	1
CRM product evaluation process	Method for evaluating CRM solutions	1
Offline usage with synchronization	Offline usage with synchronization by the sales force	1

Risk Total   54
40–66 Low risk
67–93 Moderate risk
94–120 High risk

References

Hammer, M and Champy, J A (1994) *Reengineering the Corporation: A manifesto for business revolution*, HarperBusiness, London

Lefébure, R and Venturi, G (2001) *Gestion de la Relation Client* [Customer Relationship Management], Eyrolles, Paris

MacHale, D (1997) *Wit*, Prion Books, London

Siragher, N (2001) *Carving Jelly*, Chiltern Publishing International, Bucks

Trout, J and Rivkin, S (1999) *The Power of Simplicity*, McGraw-Hill, Berkeley, CA

Further reading

Asselin, G and Mastron, R (2001) *Au Contraire: Figuring out the French*, Intercultural Press, Yarmouth, ME

Hall, E and Hall, M (1990) *Understanding Cultural Differences: Germans, French and Americans*, Intercultural Press, Yarmouth, ME

Storti, C (2001) *Old World, New World*, Intercultural Press, Yarmouth, ME

Trompenaars, F and Hampden-Turner, C (1997) *Riding the Waves of Culture*, Nicholas Brealey Publishing, London

WEB SITES

www.crmdaily.com
www.crm-forum.com
www.crmguru.com
www.destinationcrm.com
www.eccs.uk.com
www.jimnovo.com

Index